PUBLICATION OF THE AMERICAN DIALECT SOCIETY

Number 13

A WORD-LIST FROM "BILL ARP" AND "RUFUS SANDERS"

By

MARGARET GILLIS FIGH

COMMENTS ON WORD-LISTS IN *PADS*

By

JAMES NATHAN TIDWELL

A WORD-LIST FROM SOUTHERN KENTUCKY

By

A. P. DALTON

THE SECRETARY'S REPORT

Published by the

AMERICAN DIALECT SOCIETY

April, 1950

Obtainable from the Secretary of the Society

Woman's College of the

University of North Carolina

Greensboro, North Carolina

Continued on Cover 3

PUBLICATION OF THE AMERICAN DIALECT SOCIETY

/ 2 7

Number 13

A WORD-LIST FROM
"BILL ARP" AND "RUFUS SANDERS"

By

MARGARET GILLIS FIGH

COMMENTS ON WORD-LISTS IN *PADS*

By

JAMES NATHAN TIDWELL

A WORD-LIST FROM
SOUTHERN KENTUCKY

By

A. P. DALTON

THE SECRETARY'S REPORT

Published by the

AMERICAN DIALECT SOCIETY

April, 1950

Obtainable from the Secretary of the Society
Woman's College of the
University of North Carolina
Greensboro, North Carolina

A WORD-LIST FROM "BILL ARP" AND "RUFUS SANDERS"

MARGARET GILLIS FIGH

Huntingdon College

The following word-list was culled from the writings of two cracker barrel columnists whose works reflect the everyday speech of Georgians and Alabamians during the latter half of the nineteenth century. Because these men were contemporaries who used similar methods and many of the same expressions, it seems appropriate to combine their dialect words into one list.

"Bill Arp" (Charles H. Smith) began writing in the early 1860's and continued contributing his weekly letters to the Atlanta *Constitution* until his death in 1903. These letters were copied in numerous small papers and from time to time were published in book form. Arp first adopted the personality of a Georgia Cracker, but he soon slipped into the more congenial guise of a rural, middle-class land owner and farmer, whose colloquial language and homely philosophy contributed largely to his popularity. He is of interest today primarily because he has preserved folk customs and dialect which otherwisely might have been lost.

Francis Barto Lloyd, who wrote under the pseudonym of "Rufus Sanders" and was greatly influenced by Arp, turned to the back country of Alabama for his material. His weekly columns appeared in the Montgomery *Advertiser* throughout a period of approximately ten years until his death in 1897, after which a number of his sketches were collected in a book, *Sketches of Country Life*. This obscure volume and the columns in the files of the *Advertiser* contain a surprising amount of regional lore and language as well as many tall tales and much local imagery. Lloyd was born in the village of Mount Willing, Loundes County, Alabama, and spent all his life in this and adjoining counties. He had an unusually keen ear and an appreciation of the local color which prevailed in his section during his own time, and he was also interested in that of an earlier generation, whose customs, anecdotes, and folk wisdom he delighted in recording.

The word-list which follows presents examples of the dialect used by Arp and Sanders. All of the sayings were taken from Sanders's works.

3

EDITOR'S NOTE

When there may be some doubt as to the pronunciation of a word, Mrs. Figh gives the current pronunciation, which is probably that used by "Arp" and "Sanders." She is unacquainted with the pronunciation of some words, and makes no attempt to indicate it.

Works given in the bibliography below are the sources of the glossary and sayings. Immediately after a bibliographical entry is placed the abbreviated form of the title used with each citation.

BIBLIOGRAPHY

LLOYD, BARTO. *Sketches of Country Life*, Press of Roberts & Son, Birmingham, 1898. *Sketches.*

————. "Rufus Sanders," Files of *The Montgomery Advertiser* from 1888 to 1897. *Advertiser.*

SMITH, CHARLES H. *Bill Arp's Scrap Book, Humor and Philosophy*, J. P. Harrison & Co., Atlanta, 1884. *Scrap Book.*

———— *Bill Arp, So Called, A Side Show of the Sunny Side of the War*, Metropolitan Record Office, New York, 1886. *Side Show.*

———— *The Farm and the Fireside*, The Constitution Publishing Company, Atlanta, 1890. *Farm.*

———— *Memorial Edition, 1861–1903*, The Hudgins Company, Atlanta, 1903. *Memorial.*

———— "Bill Arp's Weekly Letters" from the files of *The Atlanta Constitution* and other papers cited in context. *Letters.*

A. GLOSSARY

beat bobtail: *adv. phr.* Exceedingly; enthusiastically. An expression indicating emphatic action. "Blev Scroggins was mixin around among the various delegates to *beat bobtail*." *Sketches*, 46.

big lazies: *n.* Disinclination to work. "He want worth his weight in sap sawdust, and the general wonderment was that he could have the *big lazies* continually all the time and keep out of the poor house." *Sketches*, 21.

big lazy: *adj.* Very indolent. "Sometimes I would get good tired and *big lazy* and swear eternal disgust for the farm." *Sketches*, 204.

big rich: *adj.* Very wealthy. "Well, my brother Ben lives over there and he's got *big rich*, and no family, and I thought if you'd see him and tell him how sorry we was gettin' along he mout do something for us." *Farm*, 181. "It ain't much probable that I will ever get *big-rich* or run for Congress. . . ." *Sketches*, 195.

brow band [brau]: *n.* Front band on trousers. "There are wrinkles under the *brow band* of my breeches as big as you are." *Sketches*, 28.

brush arbor: *n.* An arbor made of branches of trees and shrubs, used to hold church services in. "He would like for the members to build a *brush arbor* and put up plenty of seats." *Sketches*, 217.

bubby blossoms: *n. DAE*, 1791: Shrub peculiar to this province [Va.], named from custom of girls putting this shrub down their bosoms until it has lost its grateful perfume. "I may be mistaken but it seems to me a little higher grade of happiness to . . . hunt flowers and *bubby blossoms* with the children. . . ." *Farm*, 61.

buck ager ['egə]: *n. DAE:* Heart thumps and throat pricking attendant upon shooting a deer. From *ague*, a chill. Lloyd uses the term in the sense of chill with fever. "That old home feelin would creep up like a *buck ager* then wear off about the same way." *Sketches*, 14.

bug: *v. t.* To cheat or deceive. ". . . the pritty little pullet was sent to her to kinder even for the way in which she got *bugged* when she took old Lige in out of the weather." *Sketches*, 51.

buntin hen: *n.* Among the Negroes of Dallas County, Ala., a buntin' hen is a hen without a tail, or a rumpless hen. The term is probably derived from *bunty*, which *DAE* defines as a tailless fowl. "I think the *buntin hen* is setting somewhere, and there's six eggs in my drawer that old Browny laid on my bed." *Farm*, 87.

calico corner, in the: *phr.* Among the girls and women. ". . . I never took a stand and made my final resting place around *in the calico corner*, but when them two town girls come and picked me for a native born idiot. . . ." *Sketches*, 25.

chunk: *n.* A thickset animal. *DAE* gives the definition with horse or pony. "Cobe has a *chunk* of a cow and a sow and pig. . . . *Farm*, 93.

comfort: *n.* Pleasure; amusement. "His special *comfort* was a circus." *Farm*, 29.

copperas breeches: *n.* and *adj. DAE:* Home-spun breeches dyed green. "By this time some of the folks at home had fixed me up with a pair of new *copperas breeches* for Sunday." *Sketches*, 249.

done gone clean dead: *vb. phr.* To be crazy, stultified. "I say, Gim, is you *done gone clean dead?*" *Farm*, 235.

crop: *v. t.* To plant or make a crop. "Our nearest neighbor *cropped* it over some seven hundred acres of scattering land, situated from six to ten inches under water." *Side Show*, 95.

cut a curf: *phr.* To make a show. "The trouble with most men is that they sail in to make money and *cut a big curf* and don't have time to make a living." *Sketches*, 136.

dick-nailing: See *ring-tail, dick-nailing.*

dog-poor: *adj.* Poverty stricken. "The Lucases were big rich, whilst the Simkinses were *dog poor.*" *Advertiser*, Sept. 9, 1895, 15.

do-nothing: *adj.* Lazy. "She knows what care is and work is, and one of these *do-nothing* women can't stand it." *Farm*, 81.

drean [drin]: *v. t.* To drain; to empty. "The preacher *dreaned* the gourd and returned his thanks to the boy." *Sketches*, 34.

dry drouth: *n.* and *adj.* A tautology. ". . . them snakes I've been killin' brought all this *dry drouth* in my land and ruined my crop." *Scrap Book*, 176.

family room: *n.* Usually the bedroom of the mistress of the house, where there was always a fire in contrast to the parlor, which was heated only on special occasions. "We've got a great big fire-place in the *family room*, and can boil the coffee or heat a kettle of water on the hearth if we want to, for we are not always on the lookout for company all the time like we used to be." *Farm*, 60.

flat-boat preacher: *n.* Bill Arp explained that a flat-boat preacher was of "a rough and tumble lot who peddled and preached up and down rivers . . . and tied up for the double purpose of preaching and selling whiskey." *Letters, Centreville Press*, June 19, 1902.

flugens ['flud ʒıns]: *n. DAE: Flugens* has the force of *the dickens.* "It was cold as the *flugens* that day." *Sketches*, 31.

fly bonnet: *n.* A bonnet with a ruffle or diagonal extension to the shoulder and usually made over pasteboard slats. "She tore off . . . with her *fly bonnet* in one hand. *Sketches*, 176.

fresh married: *phr.* Recently married. "Gray Dick, our old shawl-neck rooster, had come around and stood on the front door step last Tuesday mornin and crowed loud and long and mannish like he was right *fresh married* to the loveliest pullet in the settlement." *Sketches*, 263.

freshing: *adj.* Raining hard. "And it ain't done *freshin'* yet, for the frogs are croakin' and the camphor bottle is cloudy." *Scrap Book*, 139.

fried shirt: *n.* Stiffly starched shirt. "And then you can see some good old brother . . . with his store bought clothes and his *fried shirt* on. . . ." *Sketches*, 135.

gal boy: *n.* An effiminate boy. "I reckon no doubt by this time you have seen a few '*gal boys*,' as Aunt Nancy Newton calls them, but I ruther like a real, genuine, natural, healthy boy—one that can travel all the gaits and cover all the ground." *Sketches*, 30.

Gatlins, by: *interj.* Mild expletive with the force of *by George.* ". . .but *by Gatlins*, when you want to hear . . . you can always send for me. . . ." *Sketches*, 107.

gimlety: *adj.* Skinny; thin; sharp; like a gimlet. "They'll be picayunish and nice and sharp featured and *gimlety*. . . ." *Farm*, 158.

go snooks: *vb. phr.* Each person pay the same amount. "They had *went snooks* to buy the dog, and each man owned an undivided one-third interest in him." *Sketches* 279.

gobbler: *n.* A large and rough looking man. "When he got on the cars he took a seat and set down next to me. He was a long tall *gobbler*. . ." *Sketches*, 80.

golnation: *adj.* A substitute for *damned* or some other profane word. "But I am getting *golnation* tired of waitin, Rufus." *Sketches*, 69.

grunty: *adj.* Feeling bad; complaining. "When a man who ain't no yearlin gets married . . . he sets on the piazza, tired and *grunty*. . . ." *Farm*, 151.

high-heel good time: *phr.* An exciting, gay time. "And it did look to me like of all discovered places . . . for a youngster to go and have a *high-heel good time* that was the mainest place." *Sketches*, 249.

hook or mercrook, by: *adv. phr.* Variation of *by hook or crook. Jacker mer lantern* and *thingermerjig* are two comparable expressions widely used in the South. "But it so happened *by* some *hook or mercrook* that he hadn't been takin any hand in the races that week." *Sketches*, 139.

hoppin-bug: *n.* The cricket. "The *hoppin-bug* chirruped on the hearth." *Side show*, 124.

keep the smoke house greasy: *phr.* To have food in the larder; to provide plenty to eat. "It's well enough to have book learning . . . still it takes a leetle bit more solid and substantial like to *keep the smoke house greasy* and meet the general store account." *Advertiser*, May 21, 1893.

kerdo [kə'du]: *n.* Ado; bustle. "But you go right on sawin on that old fiddle and runnin off to every picnic and *kerdo* you can hear of." *Sketches*, 22.

killikinick: *n. DAE:* Sumach leaves, which mixed with tobacco, emit a delightful odor. "Calmly and cooly we smoked our *killi-kinick.*" *Farm*, 32.

lazy Lazarus: *n.* Heat waves which form an optical illusion. "When you see old *lazy Lazarus* tremblin like a ghost or spirit, risin from the ground before you . . . now that's the time for fishin." *Sketches*, 73.

leg-weary: *adj.* Tired from walking. "I was jaded and *leg-weary.*" *Sketches*, 33.

lick log: *n.* Home. Lloyd's use of this expression differs from that given in *DAE*, which cites *to stand up to one's lick log*, meaning to meet an unpleasant duty fairly and fully. Lloyd uses it generally to mean one's dwelling place. "When I got back to the old family *lick log*, I found things powerfully changed around." *Sketches*, 15.

mercrook: See *hook or mercrook, by.*

oilcloth: *n.* Rain coat. "So I put on the *oilcloth* and fooled round for an umbrel. . . ." *Farm*, 83.

overcrop: *v. t.* and *v. i.* To undertake too much. "General Hunter tried it your way and *overcropped* himself." *Side Show*, 27.

parching: *adj.* Drying; drouth-producing. "The locust is singing a *parching* tune. Summer flies keep the cows' tails busy, and all nature gives sign of a comin' drouth." *Farm*, 105.

peckerwood nubbins: *n.* Inferior corn. In the South a small portable sawmill is called a *peckerwood* sawmill. ". . .We concluded that . . . he might make a peck to the acre of *peckerwood nubbins.*" *Side Show*, 93.

pike: *v. i.* To travel on a road (pike). "And when Lou Watson come *pikin* along the big road . . . the onliest thing for me to do was to go out there and see who it was and what they wanted." *Sketches*, 27.

pistareen letter: *n.* A letter costing a pistareen to mail. In speaking of a pistareen letter, Arp explained: "A *pistareen* was 18¾ cents—that is seven pence and a thrip. We had no dimes or half dimes. The dollar was cut up in eighths instead of tenths." *Scrap Book*, 244.

plug the bull's eye: *phr.* To get the facts correctly. "I am *plugging the bull's eye* along there, stranger." *Advertiser*, May 8, 1893, 13.

rantankerous: *adj.* Cantankerous; quarrelsome. "But all them that have scraped an acquaintance with her can tell you that she

is red-headed and *rantankerous* and come from fightin stock."
Sketches, 176.

ring-tail, dicknailing: *adjs.* Emphatic epithets, usually with an
unpleasant connotation. "Squire Rogers jumped on him with a
ring-tail, dick-nailing reply." *Advertiser*, Sept. 11, 1892, 10.

rippit: *n.* A noise; confusion. "I never heard of such a *rippet* as
they kept up." *Scrap Book*, 97.

rolly-holey ['rolɪ]: *n.* A game played by rolling a ball into holes.
". . . playing town ball, bull pen, and cat and *rolly-holey* and knucks
and sweepstakes." *Memorial*, 327.

saw gourds: *phr.* To snore. "When the day's work is done . . .
he can draw his bobtail night shirt about him . . . knowin' that while
he sleeps and dreams and *saws gourds*, his worldly possessions are
growin'. . ." *Sketches*, 188.

shawl-necked rooster: *n.* and *adj.* A rooster with long feathers
giving the effect of a shawl on his neck. "Gray Dick, our old
shawl-neck rooster, had come around. . ." *Sketches*, 263.

shifty: *adj.* Most energetic; frugal. "I come down from a trading
stock of *shifty*, thrifty people. . . ." *Sketches*, 28. "I can point out
two of the *shiftiest* men in Rocky Creek settlement—men that are
clever and honest and good citizens in a general way. . . ." *Ibid.*,
105.

show smart: *phr.* To show off or exhibit oneself. "Rube rode a
flea bitten gray that had been taught to dance and prance around
and go sideways—'jest to *show smart*,' as the boys said—and it
took the animal sometime to be convinced that dancing and
prancing wasn't in order at this particular time." *Farm*, 14.

shuck basket: *n.* A basket made of corn shucks. "A little one-
horse concern containeth . . . my worldly possessions, consisting of
. . . a *shuck basket* full of some second-class vittels." *Side Show*, 123.

shuck riddle: *n.* A device for shredding or tearing up corn
shucks. ". . . and the corn looks like the blades had been drawn
through a *shuck riddle*. *Farm*, 83.

sing low: *n.* To keep quiet. "Now let me advise you to *sing low*
about this fighting business." *Side Show*, 47.

slickery: *adj.* Slippery. "Yes, I'll be dadburned if I wouldn't have
got him, but the dinged thing was so alfred *slickery*." *Farm*, 13.

snipshus: *adj. DAE:* Smart; spruce. "He was too *snipshus* and
smart alecky, anyway." *Sketches*, 224.

sperits-of-cats-a-fightin: *n.* Whiskey. "But I have seen three or four women of my day and generation which could wean a man away from 'white ink' or *sperits-of-cats-a-fightin*." *Sketches*, 257.

stump sucker: *n.* A horse that chews wood, such as hitching posts or fences. The word is commonly used in central Alabama. "The plaintiff sued for damages because the horse was a *stump sucker* and wouldn't work on the off side." *Letters, Centreville Press*, Sept. 19, 1901.

sweetie bread: *n.* Cake-like bread. "But the cupboard want locked up, and there was a big bowl of clabber and a hunk of *sweetie bread* settin on the bottom shelf." *Sketches*, 63.

swivel: *r. t.* and *v. i.* To shrivel; to shrink. "Sometimes I think to myself if Christmas didn't come regular onest a year . . . this old world would soon *swivel*, and swink up and die with the dry rots." *Sketches*, 155. "I . . . filled my pockets full of scalybarks and peanuts and some *swivelled* up apples of my own raisin." *Ibid.*, 53.

talk-or-bust: *adj.* Unable to keep a secret. "Gus is the *talk-or-bust* sort of man." *Advertiser*, Sept. 11, 1892, 10.

tew: *v. t.* To tease; to quiz. "Then they let into picking and *tewin* at Andy about this, that and the other jest to see how bad he had muddled and mixed up with himself." *Sketches*, 146.

thanky-bag: *n.* A bag used by women for carrying odds and ends, tobacco, etc. The term probably originated from the custom of stowing small gifts in this bag. "Aunt Nancy put her pipe away in her *thanky bag*. . . ." *Sketches*, 136.

thrash pole: *n.* A large switch. "I'll stratin you out with a *thrash pole* till you can't see." *Letters, Clark County Democrat*, April 8, 1873. The expression is still used by the mountain people.

tighteye thickets: *n.* Hedge-like shrubs growing in swamps. "He had jest simply been roaming round and round . . . plungin and tearin through cane brakes and *tighteye thickets* till you mought think he had rid a whirlwind through Cyclone Streak." *Sketches*, 267.

trampoose: *v. i. DAE:* To tramp or trudge through. Arp uses the word in the sense of to wander about or stroll. "He . . . began *trampoosing* around and every little crowd he got to, he would lean forward in an insolent manner and say, 'Anybody got anything agin Ben McGinnis?'" *Farm*, 23.

tread saft: *n. DAE:* 1814: Tread softly; spurge nettle. "Then there is briars and nettles and *tread safts* and smartweed and poison oak . . . that's always in the way on a farm and must be looked after keerfully." *Farm,* 58.

weaving way: *n.* State of excitement. "Oncst upon a time a powerful young preacher come . . . and held a meeting over at Bark Log . . . and when he got into one of his *weavin ways,* he could fairly make your hair curl and your blood run cold." *Sketches,* 281.

whet: *n.* Amount; space; time. "You have lived a long *whet.*" *Advertiser,* July 5, 1896. 4.

white ink: *n.* Whiskey. Andy Lucas "takes to *white ink* like an orphant kitten to a pan of sweet milk." *Advertiser,* July 15, 1894, 5.

willipus wallipus: *n.* Something with which to frighten or alarm, i.e., a bogey man. In central Alabama the term is now applied to big, ungainly machines like those used in road making. "I have humored and indulged them until they think there is no *willipus wallipus* on the plantation." *Farm,* 325.

word out, be or **put:** *phr.* To be announced to announce. He "was planning to marry someone else at the same time his *word was out* with Rosebud." *Advertiser,* May 14, 1893.

B. SAYINGS

Not to know from **Adam's off ox.** (Not to recognize one.) "He didn't know me from Adam's off ox." *Advertiser,* May 6, 1894, 8.

To shed one's **baby teeth.** (To be sophisticated; not easily deceived.) "I've done shed my baby teeth." *Advertiser,* Dec. 2, 1894, 2.

To **beat** six bits. "Cis Bradley was drinkin' . . . carryin' on to beat six bits." *Advertiser,* March 21, 1897, 8.

Like **bees** around a molasses jug. (Crowded thickly.) ". . . the girls they clustered round me like bees around a molasses jug." *Sketches,* 250.

Big enough to knock a cow down. (Vary large.) *Sketches,* 145.

Not much **bigger** than a pound of soap after a hard day's washing. *Advertiser,* April 28, 1895, 2.

Than a **blind calf** in a cane brake. "You won't stand anymore showin' than a blind calf in a cane brake." *Advertiser,* August 13, 1893, 13.

Like a **blind calf** in high oats. (Unable to do anything or to act intelligently; in an impossible position.) "Take one of your real, regular newspaper fellows and drop him down on a first-class well-regulated farm, and he would be like a blind calf in high oats." *Sketches*, 203.

Than a **blind steer** in a stampede. ". . . A weaklin' didn't stand no more showin' in Texas than a blind steer in a stampede." *Advertiser*, July 16, 1893, 14.

Like a **bobtail dog** at a log walkin.' (Hopelessly handicapped.) "He would be like a bobtail dog at a log walkin'. *Sketches*, 203.

To **bog** the shadow of a buzzard. "The road was sloppy enough to bog the shadow of a buzzard." *Sketches*, 285.

"He was **born** in a hurry and died the same way." *Sketches*, 191.

Bull of the woods. (Leader; master.) "In those days Blev Scroggins wore the bell and called himself bull of the woods." *Advertiser*, May 6, 1894, 8.

Bull-proof and pig-tight. (Giving perfect security; impregnable.) "An old man had a mortgage on his land that was 'bull-proof and pig-tight.'" *Advertiser*, March 17, 1895, 2.

It is plenty time to **burn** down the bridge after you git across the creek. (Burn your bridges behind you—not before you.) *Sketches*, 208.

To **burn** up a mill pond. (A variant of *to set the world on fire*.) "I don't think you will ever burn up anybody's mill pond, nor either go to Congress." *Sketches*, 222.

As **busy** as forty thousand bees in a tar bucket. *Sketches*, 109.

"To go up like a **cat's back**." (To rise quickly as the cat's back does when the animal is angry.) "The price of corn went up like a cat's back." *Sketches*, 245.

Chew your own tobacco. (Rely on yourself.) "Chew your own tobacco. Hold your head up. Look the sun in the face." *Sketches*, 202.

You can't **churn** butter from the milk that is spilt. (Similar to *There is no use crying over spilt milk*.) *Sketches*, 208.

For a **clear deed** to a ten-acre lot in Heaven. "I wouldn't take a drink for a clear deed to a ten-acre lot in Heaven." *Sketches*, 261.

As **cold** as a cucumber. *Advertiser*, Dec. 9, 1896, 2.

There are no **colt's teeth** in my mouth. (I am not young and foolish.) "I am no spring chicken and neither are there any colt's teeth in my mouth." *Advertiser*, Oct. 9, 1892.

"A **craw full** of sand." Plenty of courage. "Now Sam Nettles was a man with only a few words, but a craw full of sand." *Sketches*, 55.

As **crazy** as seventeen fools. *Sketches*, 158.

Like a **deer** in a walk. "You can win like a deer in a walk." *Advertiser*, Aug. 13, 1893, 13.

"As **easy** as falling off a log." *Advertiser*, Jan. 3, 1897, 7.

"As **easy** as falling off a greasy log." *Ibid.*, Jan. 14, 1894, 8.

As **easy** as picking it up in the big road. "You can git the office as easy as pickin' it up in the big road." *Advertiser*, Aug. 13, 1893, 13.

"But the **eggs** wouldn't hatch out that way." (Plans or desires were not carried out.) *Advertiser*, May 6, 1894, 8.

Fight one's weight in wildcats. "Aunt Nancy Newton would fight her weight in wildcats." *Advertiser*, June 21, 1896, 2.

Fighting like a pair of mangy dogs over a soup bone. *Sketches*, 130.

"As **free** as water running down hill." *Sketches*, 260.

"Like a **free nigger** in a hen roost." *Advertiser*, May 6, 1894, 8.

Like **fur** on a cat's back. "Your hair will stand up like the fur on a cat's back when a new dog comes into the kitchen." *Advertiser*, Dec. 16, 1894, 15.

Fits to a **gnat's heel.** "The name fits the man to a gnat's heel." *Advertiser*, March 14, 1897, 9.

It suited me to a **gnat's heel.** *Advertiser*, May 7, 1893, 8.

"As **happy** as a dead pig in the sunshine." *Sketches*, 75.

Harder than a mule could kick with both feet. "I loved her ten times harder than a mule could kick with both feet." *Sketches*, 74.

A **head** on one's shoulders as long as a flour barrel. *Sketches*, 221.

As **high** as a cat's back. "The Lucas generation got their dander up as high as a cat's back." *Advertiser*, Sept. 9, 1894.

Hungry enough to eat a mule. "I was hungry enough to eat a mule, hair hide, and all." *Sketches*, 61.

Lousy with money. (Very rich.) "Plum louzy with money." *Advertiser*, Jan. 14, 1893, 7.

As **meek** and mild as a sore-eyed kitten on a fresh ash bank. *Advertiser*, Dec. 2, 1894, 2.

To put one's **mudhooks** on slippery ground. (To be uncertain;

to be unable to grasp.) "But when a farmer goes to foolin' with figgers he is puttin' his mudhooks on powerful slippery ground." *Sketches*, 239.

As **plain** as a painted horse rack. "The whole thing sticks out as plain to me as a painted horse rack." *Advertiser*, May 6, 1894, 7.

As **plain** as a white-washed fence around a graveyard. *Advertiser*, Sept. 9, 1894.

As **pretty** as red shoes with blue stockings. *Advertiser*, Sept. 9, 1894.

Pull up the bush. (To outdo all others; to win the prize.) "As a quitter . . . Lige Runnels would take the rag and pull up the bush over any man in the Rocky Creek settlement." *Sketches*, 183.

Regular as pig tracks. *Advertiser*, May 6, 1849, 8.

Like a man who didn't put any **salt** in his dirt. (Salt is considered necessary to make a big, strong man.) "He stood about six feet and three axe handles in his socks and looked like a man that didn't put any salt in his dirt." *Sketches*, 31.

To have a **seat** in the amen corner when the brains are passed around. (To be intelligent.) "She didn't have a seat on a front bench in the amen corner when they passed around the brains." *Sketches*, 278.

Like a **seed tick** to a nigger's shin. *Sketches*, 179.

To **set** one's triggers. (To make plans.) "I've been settin' my triggers to get him and the widder Motes in the same trap." *Advertiser*, Sept. 11, 1892.

Like a **shedding rooster** after a rainstorm. (In a dilapidated condition.) "The old farm . . . puts me in mind of a sheddin' rooster after a rainstorm." *Sketches*, 204.

"There's many a **slippance** between the spring down under the hill and the bucket on the water shelf." (Variant of *There's many a slip twixt cup and lip*.) *Advertiser*, Sept. 11, 1892, 8.

Small potatoes and few in the hill. (Insignificant; of little importance.) "To be plain and honest about it, we men folks are generally mighty small potatoes and blame few in the hill, anyhow." *Sketches*, 19.

As **snug** as a meadow mouse under a fodder stack. "I can . . . go to sleep as neat and as snug as a meadow mouse under a fodder stack." *Sketches*, 195.

As **soft** as the fur on a cat's back. *Advertiser*, Jan. 3, 1897, 7.

To **spit** on the slate and start over. (To erase one's former mistakes and begin again.) "If I could only spit on the slate and spile out and start over I would save myself from many of the trials . . . I have been through." *Sketches*, 200.

To **stick** in one's craw. (To irritate or anger anyone.) ". . .but it stuck in his craw powerful to think that old Sol Simkinses boy had won the race in a canter. . ." *Sketches*, 223.

To **swim** without gourds. (To be self-reliant.) This expression arose from the custom of boys' using gourds to hold themselves up while learning to swim. "You must. . .stand up and walk like a man, swim without gourds." *Sketches*, 201.

"**Take** the rag." (A variant of *take the cake;* to win the prize.) "As a quitter I reckon maybe Lige Runnels would take the rag and pull up the bush over any man in Rocky Creek settlement." *Sketches*, 183.

As **thick** as four in a bed. (Friendly; affectionate.) "We was born the same day. . .and came up neck and neck together. Tom Dick's ma used to say we was as thick as four in a bed." *Sketches*, 219.

"He has. . .got you where the **tick** had the steer calf." *Advertiser*, May 6, 1894, 8.

Tote your own skillet. (Be self-reliant; a variant of *Paddle your own canoe*.) "Tote your own skillet and take things easy. . . .Let the Sanders tub set on its own bottom first, last and for evermore." *Sketches*, 199.

As **ugly** as a chop axe. (Very ugly.) *Sketches*, 242.

As **ugly** as a meat axe. *Advertiser*, March 8, 1896, 2.

Ugly enough to wean a mule colt. *Advertiser*, Feb. 4, 1894, 11.

"**Withered** like a Sunday shirt in August." *Sketches*, 76.

Not to be **worth** one's weight in sap sawdust. (To be utterly useless.) "He had been petted and spoiled till he want worth his weight in sap sawdust." *Sketches*, 200.

Get the **wrong sow** by the ear. "He got the wrong sow by the ear." *Advertiser*, May 7, 1893, 8.

Like a **yearling calf** with the hollow horn. (Acting like one sick.) "I couldn't do nothin' but go creepin' and mopin' around like a yearlin' calf with the hollow horn." *Sketches*, 13.

COMMENTS ON WORD-LISTS IN *PADS*

JAMES NATHAN TIDWELL

San Diego State College

Many of the words and expressions which have appeared in previous *PADS* are known to me from my boyhood years in Runnels County, Texas (1911–1929), and from my regular visits there since 1929. Because the definition or pronunciation of the words or the form of the expressions in *PADS* did not always coincide with Runnels County speech, I have made the following comments on variants in definition, pronunciation, or form, adding also some illustrative quotations from written sources. The number of *PADS* and the page number of the original entry are given in parentheses immediately after each entry here.

A. GLOSSARY

amen corner: *n.* (2:24) That part of the church, usually the front seats on the left or right, where the staunchest members sit and say "Amen." The middle front seat is kept open for those "under conviction" and is known as the *mourner's bench*.

back-talk: *n.* (6:5) The verb form is *talk back*. "Did he *talk back* to you?"

bait: *n.* (2:53) A quantity, not necessarily large. "We had a *bait* of turnips." Cf. R. Head and F. Kirkman, *The English Rogue* (1665–71, reprinted 1928), pp. 351–2: "But at noon-day staying for a *bait*, I happened into the company of a trooper, who was likewise travelling to London. We dined together. . . ."

blind-bridle: *n.* (6:6) A bridle having blinders. Always used on work horses; never used on saddle horses; used on buggy horses only when their skittishness will not permit the use of an *open-bridle*.

booger: *vb.* (2:28) To commit sodomy; also to disfigure, as the threads of a bolt. "He *boogered* it up."

bottom, bottoms: *n.* (5:12) A stretch of low land along a river or stream; not used for other valleys. Cf. B. Drake and E. D. Mansfield, *Cincinnati in 1826* (1827), p. 28: "The Lower Market House is situated in the *bottom*. . . ." Cf. also C. F. Hoffman, *A winter in the West* (1835), I, 57.

broomstick, to jump over the: *phr.* (2:25) To get married. Often shortened to *jump the broom*.

bundle: *n.* (5:13) Sheaf. The word *sheaf* is almost never used except in Biblical references.

cart wheel: *n.* (6:8) A handspring done to the side.

cattawampus: *adj.* (5:14) Awry. It is not synonomous with *catty-cornered*, which means diagonally or almost diagonally.

chamber: *n.* (5:14) *Chamber* in the sense of a room is known from reading, but it is not used in conversation because *chamber* is the common word for a chamber pot.

channel cat: *n.* (2:54) A fresh-water catfish which may be a *yellow channel cat* or a *blue channel cat.* The meat of the channel cat is considered tastier than that of the *mud cat.*

cock: *n.* (2:18) *Pudenda muliebra.*

corn crib: *n.* (5:16) The word *crib* is applied to a barn or a part which is built to hold threshed small grains (oats, wheat, etc.) or ears of corn.

creen: *vb.* (2:41) To bend from a natural position. "The barn is *creening* a little."

cud [kʊd]: *n.* (2:18) A chew of tobacco is called a *cud,* not a *quid.*

cut: *vb.* (5:19) To castrate. *Cut* is the common word among men, but before women, one would use *castrate* or *work on. Cut* or *cut meat* may also mean to copulate.

diddle: *vb.* (2:42) To copulate. *Diddle with,* however, means to fool with. "I wouldn't *diddle* with that if I was you."

finger— little, ling, long, lick-pot, and thumb-ball: *n.* (6:13) The form in Runnels County was *little-man*['lɪtlmən], *leeman, longman, lick-pot,* and *thumb-ball.*

flitter: *n.* (6:13) A fritter. Uneducated. However, it is almost always *flitter* in the expression "as flat as a flitter," possibly because of the alliteration.

frog: *n.* (2:9) A toad. Cf. Baldwin, *Party Leaders* (1855), p. 337: "...[banks] that had sprung up, like *frog*-stools...."

grabble: *vb.* (6:15) To catch fish with the hands.

grass, to go to: *phr.* (6:15) To be untended, as "His fields *went to grass.*" Often said to children, meaning for them to go away and amuse themselves.

gumption: *n.* (6:16) We used the word to mean common sense: "He doesn't have the *gumption* God gave a goose." But it is obviously used to mean initiative in *Time Magazine* 1 March 1948, p. 15/3: "The old git and *gumption* was no longer there."

halves, to go: *phr.* (2:57) Cf. R. Head and F. Kirkman, *The*

English Rogue (1665–71, reprinted 1928), p. 567: "Then he said he would *go halves* no longer. . . ." The schoolboys of Runnels County often said *go halvers*, a usage which appears in *Selected Letters of W. A. White* (1947), p. 112: "They can't *go halvers* with the Interests." Farmers spoke of *renting on the halves* when the rental agreement called for renter and owner to share equally.

high sign, to give the: *phr.* (2:34) To signal a message with gestures; to give a signal to go ahead.

hindside first: *adv.* (2:25) The expression among the uneducated was *hindside foremost*.

hog's head cheese: *n.* (5:26) A jellied sausage from the meat of a hog's head or feet. Pig's entrails are never used. More frequently called *souse*.

John Henry: *n.* (2:34) Never heard in the sense of a dude. A fairly common humorous name for a signature: "Put your *John Henry* to that."

laid up: *adj.* (6:19) Abed with some form of sickness, not necessarily for "a long while." "I was *laid up* on Thursday."

leader: *n.* (6:19) Any tendon, not just the tendon in the neck.

loblolly: *n.* (2:58) Any very unsightly mess, but usually a liquid one. "He made a loblolly in the kitchen."

middling: *adj.* (5:30) Often *fair to middling*. Both expressions are felt to be derived from the grading of cotton into middling, fair to middling, etc.

more than Carter has oats: *phr.* (2:58) A tremendous amount. Usually *more than Carter had oats*. Carter supposedly grew more oats than he had land to stack them on.

one o'clock: *phr.* (2:20) A euphemistic hint that one's trousers are unbuttoned. Rare in Runnels. The more common hint is, "Have you got a sore thumb, Jim?"

out: *n.* (2:47) An attempt, not necessarily an unsuccessful one. "He made a hell of an *out* of it"; "I'll make an *out* at it."

paling fence: *n.* (5:30) A fence made of pales (pointed slats) joined by wire. A picket fence is made by nailing pickets to crossmembers.

picket fence: *n.* (5:30) See *paling fence*.

possum: *vb.* (2:20) To sulk or play dead. Often also used as a noun: *playing 'possum*. Cf. F. Marryat, *A Diary in America* (1839), p. 186: ". . .Miss Martineau appears to have been what the Kentuckians call *'playing possum.'*"

pussy ['pʌsɪ]: *adj*. Pursy. Not confused with *pussy* ['pusɪ], *pudenda muliebra*.

rotgut: *n*. (2:60) Bad liquor. A speaker in an 1824 D.C. Johnston cartoon (reproduced in Nevins and Weitenkampf, *Political Cartoons*, p. 33) says: "Blast my eyes if I don't *venter* a small horn of *rotgut* on that bald filly in the middle." Cf. also G. D. Brewerton, *The War in Kansas* (1856), p. 254.

quietus: *n*. (2:48) Used only in *put a quietus to* (put an end to). Old-fashioned.

sa, madam: *phr*. (2:48) The Runnels County command to a cow to stand still is *saw, cow* [sɔ kau], or just *saw*.

scrooch: *vb*. (2:49; 5:36) To crouch. Distinct from *scroudge*, to crowd. Cf. Landon, *Eli Perkins' Wit, Humor and Pathos* (1883), p. 19: "I could see it from behind the sofa where I *scootched* down."

shank's ponies, to ride: *phr*. (2:60) To walk. The Runnels County form was *to ride shank's mares*. Cf. G. D. Brewerton, *The War in Kansas* (1856), p. 43: "*Shank's mare.*"

shock: *n*. (5:37) A stack of sheaves in the field, set up in groups of sixteen to thirty, each sheaf resting on its bottom end. Standard use. Never used for a pile of hay.

sky-windin': *adv*. (2:60) To a great height, usually over and over in the air. "He knocked me *sky-windin'*."

slop bucket: *n*. (5:38) A pail for liquid garbage. Distinct from *slop jar*, a large chamber pot.

snap the whip: *phr*. (6:27) Our form was *to crack the whip*. "Let's play *crack the whip*."

spit cotton: *phr*. (2:50; 2:55) I have heard this used only in describing the extreme dryness of the mouth which makes the spittle look like cotton.

split: *vb*. (6:28) Plowing out middles was often called *busting out middles*, but never *splitting*.

spring chicken: *n*. (6:28) A young woman. Used almost entirely in the negative: "She's no *spring chicken*." Slang. Cf. G. D. Prentice, *Prenticeana* (1871), p. 97: "Call a lady 'a chicken,' and ten to one she is angry. Tell her she is 'no chicken,' and twenty to one she is still angrier."

stove up: *adj*. (6:29) Unable to work because of illness. A horse is stove up when he is string-halted or drawn from over-work. A man is stove up when he has rheumatism or some such stiffening illness.

swivet, in a: *phr.* (6:29) In an emotional storm; in a nervous hurry. In a letter to *Time Magazine* (22 March 1948, p. 6/3), a reader asked where *Time* found the word *swivet*, which it had used in the March 1 issue. *Time* replied that it "got it from a Texan in a tizzy."

T, to a: *phr.* (6:29) Exactly. The meaning apparently comes from the exactness of a carpenter's T-square. Cf. G. D. Prentice, *Prenticeana* (1871), p. 70: ". . . even his friends must admit, that, if nature designed to make the initial of the word 'thief' upon his person and mind, she certainly 'hit it *to a T.*'"

thunder mug: *n.* (6:30) A large chamber pail. The small ones were called *chambers*.

tow sack: *n.* (5:42) Usual name for a burlap sack. Never used for a canvas sack. Cf. C. F. Hoffman, *A Winter in the West* (1835), I, 42: "They generally have a tow-cloth knapsack. . . ."

twat: *n.* (2:51) The buttocks. Taylor Co., Texas. Cf. R. Head and F. Kirkman, *The English Rogue* (1665–71, reprinted 1928), p. 312: ". . . as if they would break their very twatling strings therewith."

week, (Tuesday) was a week ago: *phr.* (2:14) Cf. *Georgia Journal* (Milledgeville, Ga.) 14 Sept. 1841, p. 3/2: ". . . *Saturday was a week ago.*"

B. SAYINGS

Well, this ain't buying the **baby** any clothes. (6:34) In Runnels Co.: *This ain't making the baby any clothes.*

I'll give you the next **dime** I find in a sheep's track. (2:22) In Runnels Co.: . . . *in an elephant's track.*

To ride a **high horse.** (6:38) Much more usual in Runnels was *to be on a high horse.* "He's on a high horse today."

As **homely** as a mud-fence. (2:57) Never heard with *homely*, but *as ugly as a mud-fence* is heard frequently.

I'll make you **laugh** on the other side of your face. (6:39) Cf. R. Head and F. Kirkman, *The English Rogue* (1665-71, reprinted 1928), p. 571: ". . . being brothers of a trade and both served alike, they resolved to laugh too, though it were but with one side of their mouths. . . ."

If your **nose** itches, company is coming. (6:40) The Runnels Co. version was: *My nose itches; Someone's coming with a hole in his britches.*

To take one down a **notch** or two. (6:41) Frequent, but no more common than *to take one down a button-hole*. Cf. R. Head and F. Kirkman, *The English Rogue*, (1665–71, reprinted 1928), p. 566: "... he was taken down a button-hole lower...."

As **smart** as a Philadelphia lawyer. (6:42) Cf. J. K. Paulding, *Letters from the South* (1817), II, 44: "... puzzle a Philadelphia lawyer"; G. D. Brewerton, *The War in Kansas* (1856), p. 106; and J. K. Paulding, *John Bull in America* (1825), pp. 163–4.

If you can't **talk,** shake a bush. (6:42) If you can't talk, shake your head.

Ugly enough to stop an eight-day clock. (6:43) The West Texas version is, "His face would stop a clock." Cf. *Time Magazine* 26 April 1948, p. 14/3, which reports a Chicago woman as saying, "I always knew your face would stop a clock."

A WORD-LIST FROM SOUTHERN KENTUCKY

A. P. DALTON

Holland, Kentucky

acause [ə'kɔz] : *conj.* Because. Heard occasionally among uneducated. Found in the dialects of Cumberland, York, and Lancaster shires. "Why did you do that?" "Jist *acause*."

afeard : *adj.* Afraid. Fairly common among uneducated. "I hain't *afeard* to go by a graveyard after dark. "Cf. Pepys, *Diary*, Sept. 5, 1666: "I became *afeard* to stay there long. . . ." Chaucer, Prologue to the *Canterbury Tales*, 628: "Of his visage children were *aferd*." *Everyman*, 251: "Also it make[s] me *aferde*, certayne."

baste [best] : *v. t.* To beat, strike. A survival of the Old Norse verb *beyasta*, "to beat." "I'll *baste* you on the head with a rock."

blow up : *v. t.* Of weather: to change for the worse. "Hit looks like hit might *blow up* cold tonight." Cf. *The Rape of Lucrece*, 1788: "This windy tempest, till it *blow up* rain."

brang [bræŋ] : Present tense of *bring*. This pronunciation is rather common among the uneducated. Found also among the dialects of Dorset and Somerset shires. "What did ye *brang* me from town?"

brethern : *n. Brethren.* See *sistern.*

chanct : *n., v. t.,* and *v. i. Chance.* Fairly common among uneducated. "I never had a *chanct* t' go t' school when I was agrowin' up."

childern : *n. Children. Purty* and *prespire* are other examples of metathesis. Quite common among the uneducated.

clew : *n.* A ball of yarn used for darning or knitting; also a ball of hair rolled up at the nape of a woman. "Grandma takes her *clew* o' yarn and knits when she goes visitin'."

culbert : *n. Culvert. B* is substituted for *v* in this word and some other words: *Calvert, rivet,* etc. *Marble,* however, becomes *marvel.*

fire-new : *adj. Fire-new, brand-new, brand-fire-new, spit-fire-new* are all fairly common. "Jim driv in his *spit-fire-brand-new* car this evenin'." Cf. *Love's Labour's Lost*, I, i, 175: "Armado is a man of *fire-new* words." *Twelfth Night*, III, ii, 23: "*Fire-new* from the mint."

guardeen : [gɑr'din] : *n. Guardian.* Very common. Found also in the dialects of Cumberland and Dorset shires. "Her *guardeen* gits t' keep her money till she comes of age."

neb [nɛb]: *n.* An Old English relic meaning the "features of the face," especially the nose. Rare. "Keep your *neb* out o' things that don't consarn ye!"

sang [sæŋ]: *v. t.* and *v. i.* Present tense of *sing.* This [æ] sound is also heard in *bring* (see *brang*), *drink, finger, think,* etc. Also found in the dialects of Dorset and Somerset shires. "We will now *sang* 'The Old Time Religion.'"

sech: *pron.* and *adj.* Common among uneducated. Also common in rural England. "I didn't say no *sech* thing."

sistern: *n.* Sisters. Among uneducated but rare. "Brethern and *sistern,* our text for today is. . . ." (Illiterate minister)

sperit: *n. Spirit.* Among uneducated but rare. "That filly has high *sperits.*" The adjective *high-sperited* also occurs.

spit-fire-brand-new: See *fire-new.*

squinch (up): *v. t.* and *v. i.* Variant of *squint.* Fairly common among uneducated. "Kin you look at the sun without *squinchin' up* your eyes?"

squinch-eyed: *adj.* Variant of *squint-eyed.* Fairly common among uneducated. "Sally wouldn't be so bad lookin' is she wasn't so *squinch-eyed.*"

stiddy ['stɪdɪ], **studdy** ['stʌdɪ]: *adj.* and *v. i. Steady.* Among uneducated. Also in Devon and Somerset shires. "Bill's got a *stiddy* job drivin' a truck." "*Studdy* this post while I nail it."

tetch: *n.* and *v. t. Touch.* Fairly common. Also in Devon, Somerset, and Wiltshire. "I jist dare ye t' *tetch* me."

THE SECRETARY'S REPORT

A. THE STANFORD MEETINGS

The Society met at Stanford University, California, September 9. Again two meetings were held: the conference on the dictionary of the Society, at 1:30–3:00 P. M. and the general (annual) meeting, at 3:15–4:45 P.M. By the time this issue is in print, members will have received a Report on the conference.

In the absence of the Secretary, Dr. James N. Tidwell, San Diego College, kindly substituted. The following papers were read:

1. "Transmitted and Indigenous Speechways of the Oregon Country," Randall V. Mills, University of Oregon.

2. "The Influence of Locale and Human Activity on Some Dialect Words in Colorado," Marjorie M. Kimmerle, University of Colorado.

3. "The Importance of the Study of Personal Names," Elsdon C. Smith, Evanston, Illinois. (In the absence of Mr. Smith, this paper was read by Dr. William Randel, Florida State University.)

Dr. Margaret M. Bryant and Dr. I. Willis Russell submitted reports for their respective committees. (Copies of these reports were given to the President.) The President reported on the progress of the Society's dictionary, and appointed as a dictionary planning committee the following members: F. G. Cassidy (Chairman), William Alexander, and James B. McMillan.

Dr. Bryant, Chairman of the Nominating Committee, submitted the following slate: For President, Allen Walker Read, for Vice-President, E. H. Criswell; for Secretary-Treasurer, George P. Wilson; and for member of the Executive Council, James B. McMillan. These nominees were all elected.

B. MEMBERSHIP

(As of September 9, 1949)

Last year our total membership was 514. This year it is 547. It breaks down as follows:

Life members	15
Annual members	357
Libraries	157
Exchange and complimentary	18
Total	547

Seventeen members have been dropped this year because of failure to pay dues or by request, mainly the former. The number of members added last year was the largest in the history of the Society; then the Secretary put on a special "drive" to get members.

The Society honors and thanks the following for sending us new members: Adeline C. Bartlett, Margaret M. Bryant, F. G. Cassidy, E. H. Criswell, Arthur R. Dunlap, Marjorie M. Kimmerle, Mamie J. Meredith, A. W. Read. To our president goes the honor of securing the largest number of new members—$4\frac{1}{2}$. The Secretary hastens to explain that this seeming Solomonic bisecting of one new member is due to the fact that Mr. Read and another member co-operatively influenced one person to join. The Secretary has never honored himself by reporting that he had induced men, women, and libraries to come into our camp; this business he regards as falling within his line of duty—a sort of scouring the Augean stables (nothing malevolent or malodorous intended here).

C. SPECIAL MEETING AT ANN ARBOR

On July 29 and 30 the Society met at Ann Arbor in conjunction with the Linguistic Society of America. Nine of our members read papers: Bagby Atwood, F. G. Cassidy, Alva L. Davis, Robert A. Hall, Einar Haugen, Hans Kurath, Marjorie M. Kimmerle, Raven I. McDavid, Francis L. Utley. F. G. Cassidy was secretary *pro tem.* and was responsible for arranging the program. A. W. Read presided at the meeting on the second day.

D. REPORT OF CHAIRMEN OF RESEARCH COMMITTEES

On July 14, 1949, the Secretary requested the chairmen of research committees that they send him an account of what their committees had done or expected to do during 1949. Dr. Bryant and Dr. Russell sent in reports; Dr. Bently said that he would and may have done so at the Stanford meeting, though the Secretary has not been so informed. Dr. Marckwardt sent the Secretary the following report in January, 1950:

The committee has been reconstituted as follows: Professors Henry Alexander of Queen's University, E. Bagby Atwood of the University of Texas, James B. McMillan of the University of Alabama, Raven I. McDavid of the University of Illinois, and Albert H. Marckwardt of the University of Michigan as chairman.

This year the committee has functioned principally as a clearing-house of information concerning projects in linguistic geography throughout the country. The present report is devoted chiefly to a concise summary of the present state of each of the principal projects throughout the country.

1. In May, 1949, the field work in New York State was finished by Dr. McDavid, thus completing the field work for the Middle Atlantic collection. The materials for both the Middle Atlantic and the South Atlantic states are now ready for editing. Professor Kurath has prepared a plan for editing these two collections and is attempting to secure support for such a project.

Professor Kurath's *Word Geography of the Eastern United States*, drawing upon the materials of all three coastal atlases, was published by the University of Michigan Press in November, 1949. The volume is in large format and contains 163 full page maps. Professor Atwood, with the assistance of some of his associates at the University of Texas, has prepared a word index of the *Linguistic Atlas of New England*.

2. Activity on the Linguistic Atlas of the North Central States has been concentrated in Ohio and Illinois. Research grants from Western Reserve University and the Ohio State Historical Society enabled Dr. McDavid and Professor Alva L. Davis of Western Reserve University to complete eleven field records in the two northern tiers of counties in Ohio. The University of Illinois has added Dr. McDavid to its staff with a minimum of academic duties, leaving most of his time free for field work in that state. The University has also provided him with a travel grant for this purpose.

Of the 335 field records, considered the goal for the completed North Central atlas, 173 are now in hand—slightly more than half. The addition of at least 50 records from Illinois by June, 1950, will give us two-thirds of our total at that time. Applications for further support are now pending at other institutions in the area.

3. The *Linguistic Atlas of the Upper Midwest*, under the direction of Professor Harold B. Allen of the University of Minnesota, has made substantial progress. The field work in Minnesota has been completed. Arrangements for a preliminary survey in the Dakotas are in progress with the universities in those states, and plans for a survey of Iowa are being formulated. A training course for field workers will be offered at the University of Iowa during the second semester of the current academic year.

4. An informal conference on the possibility of a *Linguistic Atlas of the Rocky Mountain States* was held in Salt Lake City on November 25, 1949, in connection with the sectional meeting of the Modern Language Association. The conference was attended by representatives of the Universities of Colorado, Utah, Denver, New Mexico, Montana State College, and various other institutions in the area. One concrete outcome of the conference is that Dr. McDavid will give a summer session course in Field Methods in Linguistic Geography at the University of Colorado in 1950.

E. GIFTS

Mrs. L. R. Dingus, widow of the late Dr. Dingus, who was one of our most valuable and beloved members, has kindly given the

Society thirty-four numbers of *Dialect Notes*. For these we are most grateful.

The Society is deeply indebted to the University of Tulsa for paying all expenses for the *The Report of the Second Conference*.

F. *Dialect Notes* AND *PADS*

Six numbers of *Dialect Notes* and one number of *PADS* had to be reprinted. The Society now has a limited number of complete sets of *Dialect Notes* and Thornton's *American Glossary*, Vol. III, and of *PADS* to date. Persons who wish to purchase sets or parts of these publications for themselves, or to have their college or university libraries do so should act at once; since reprinting is so costly, we may not have other out-of-print numbers reproduced.

G. FINANCES

Balance from 1948		$1126.32
Receipts from 1949		
Dues from persons	$464.40	
Dues from libraries	254.00	
Sale of *DN*	694.40	
Sale of *PADS*	84.60	
From Ency. Brit. Co. for new words	100.00	
Interest on money	21.99	
Total receipts		$1619.39
Total of last year's bal. and this year's receipts		$2745.71
Disbursements		
For express and postage	$19.27	
For paper and envelopes	59.70	
For postals and stamps	96.50	
For reprinting 2 numbers of *DN*	105.62	
For printing *PADS* No. 10	737.96	
For printing *PADS* No. 11	482.47	
For miscellanies	82.07	
Total disbursements		$1583.59
Balance on hand		$1162.12
Distribution of funds		
In Home Fed. & Savings Loan Assoc. of Greensboro	$1137.23	
Undeposited checks	20.00	
Undeposited cash	4.89	
Total		$1162.12

GEORGE P. WILSON
Secretary-Treasurer

THE AMERICAN DIALECT SOCIETY

Membership in the Society is conferred upon any person interested in the activities of the Society. Dues are $2.00 a year for persons or institutions. Members receive free all publications. The price of any issue when purchased separately will depend upon the production cost of the issue.

The *Publication of the American Dialect Society* is issued twice a year, in April and November.

PUBLICATION OF THE AMERICAN DIALECT SOCIETY

Number 14

A WORD-LIST FROM SOUTH CAROLINA

By

F. W. BRADLEY

EXPRESSIONS FROM RURAL FLORIDA

By

LUCILLE AYERS AND OTHERS

MINORCAN DIALECT WORDS IN ST. AUGUSTINE, FLORIDA

By

LILLIAN FRIEDMAN

Published by the

AMERICAN DIALECT SOCIETY

November, 1950

Obtainable from the Secretary of the Society

Woman's College of the

University of North Carolina

Greensboro, North Carolina

Continued on Cover 3

PUBLICATION OF THE AMERICAN DIALECT SOCIETY

Number 14

A WORD-LIST FROM SOUTH CAROLINA

By

F. W. BRADLEY

EXPRESSIONS FROM RURAL FLORIDA

By

LUCILLE AYERS AND OTHERS

MINORCAN DIALECT WORDS IN ST. AUGUSTINE, FLORIDA

By

LILLIAN FRIEDMAN

Published by the

AMERICAN DIALECT SOCIETY

November, 1950

Obtainable from the Secretary of the Society
Woman's College of the
University of North Carolina
Greensboro, North Carolina

A WORD-LIST FROM SOUTH CAROLINA

F. W. BRADLEY

University of South Carolina

A. THE NEWSPAPER AS A MEDIUM FOR DIALECT COLLECTING IN SOUTH CAROLINA

Dialect is generally understood to be at variance with standard English, and therefore to be avoided. This natural attitude on the part of the public needs to be tempered with some understanding of the fact that standard usage today is not what it was fifty years ago, nor what it will be fifty years hence, and that what was and what will be is represented in large part by dialect. Public interest can therefore be evoked by an explanation of some of the changes that language has undergone.

The excellent article of Professor George P. Wilson, "The Value of Dialect," *PADS*, No. 11, pp. 38–59, carries the message which should be made known as widely as possible to the public. There is our *raison d'être*, the justification of our labors, well suited to overcome any prejudice against dialect on the part of the public. However, as we cannot assume that the general public is familiar with this article, we must in a newspaper campaign bring that message and disarm a very real prejudice against words and expressions that are not standard. Shakespeare is a name to conjure with in this connection. Many South Carolinians pronounce the word *character* with the accent on the second syllable. Learned people smile at that. But the smile is at least more tolerant and less scornful when one remembers that the Bard of Avon did so too.

We can explain certain observable peculiarities in our speech out of the early history of our language. The well known change from the Germanic *au* to the Anglo-Saxon *ea* seems still to be in the bloodstream of the latter day Anglo-Saxons. You hear them say today: "I'm going de-an te-an [down town]." In a similar way we can throw light upon the persistent use of *ah* for *I*, the backward shift of the accent as in *invite, entire*, etc., the pronouns *hit, 'em*, etc. Scores of similar illustrations can be used to bring the public to realize that dialect is a part of our heritage as well as is standard usage.

Wide public interest is necessary if collection is to be approxi-

mately complete. Many dialect words are known and used all
over the state, many others are localized. It is needful, therefore,
to awaken a state-wide interest in collection.

The Sunday edition of the daily papers seemed to be the best
avenue of approach to the general public. We have six daily
papers with Sunday editions, the Anderson *Independent and Daily
Mail*, the Charleston *News and Courier*, the Columbia *State*, the
Florence *Morning News*, the Greenville *News*, and the Spartanburg *Herald*. Each one of these agreed to publish each Sunday
for a stated period one article of about half a column. These
journals have made our undertaking possible.

The style of such articles is of critical importance, since the
paramount aim is to attract attention and hold it. Gentlemen of
the press, Mr. Latimer of the *State* and Professor Frank Wardlaw
of the School of Journalism, were consulted on this point, and the
first article was submitted to one of them for suggestions. These
were to the point and rewarding. Such an article must be catchy
rather than erudite. A chatty style with any and all local references
available has proved fruitful.

Early articles were devoted to the double task of disarming
any prejudice that might exist against dialect and explaining our
overall plan for the dictionary and the part each state and region
has to take in carrying out the plan.

Appeal was incidentally made to the local pride and patriotism
as well as to state pride, of our readers. This is probably our strongest drawing card, since each state and each locality wishes to
take a creditable part in every general undertaking.

The pedagogical device of class participation was also applied
with excellent results. After the first article, which appeared on
the eighteenth of September, 1949, letters began to come in.
These were made the basis of future articles, with the mention
of names, except in those cases where anonymity was requested.

There was considerable discussion of what dialect is, how one
can identify it, and discriminate between dialect and slang. But
people were urged to err on the side of inclusion, and if in doubt
to send the words in. Fortunately the *New International Dictionary*
in its 1950 edition includes a large number of dialect, colloquial
and slang words, and is a guide in many cases. But not everyone
has the *NID* available, and the work of sifting falls upon the

collector. Furthermore, many words and phrases will not be found in print at all, and these are the ones we are after.

After the first two or three articles, the daily mail had more than enough material to make the next article, and so the project was well under way.

A collector should, however, not depend entirely on letters. Some people do not write letters, but they may, nevertheless, have a lively and intelligent interest in dialect. These will button-hole you on the street and tell you all about how they heard "this word." We should have a bit of pencil and a small notebook ready for them. Others will telephone you a word. We have to be prepared for all such cases, because few of us have the memory to recall accurately such reports after we get to our desk.

People of antiquarian tastes are drawn to this type of pastime, and those with good memories can recall words and their use of fifty and seventy-five years ago.

The most fruitful group of all probably were the men and women of letters. They deal in words, they have a keen sense of shades of meaning, and they remember words and their use as others remember people and their behavior.

One would expect visitors and strangers to note dialect words and expressions more readily than natives, but only a few commonplace words have come from this source. This is probably to be ascribed to the fact that strangers and visitors only frequent the shops, theaters, and hotels, all of which have more of a cosmopolitan than regional or local atmosphere.

Schools and colleges are too earnestly occupied in weeding out variations from the standard speech to pay much attention to collecting dialect. There are, however, on every faculty at least one or two members whose tastes run in our direction.

There are also in every community intelligent people who like words, who take pleasure in speculating on semantic developments, on forms and form changes, on the history of a word, and of the thought that the word represents. These are the indefatigable seekers whose interest does not flag, and who are the mainstay of a collector. Words, after all, are downright interesting.

Our articles ran weekly in the newspapers for something over six months. The newspapers had been asked for a run of only three months, but were willing to continue from September, 1949, to April of this year. We now have a large group of correspondents who can help in delimiting the area of local usages and to report on the variations in form and meaning.

The present list of words, though rather long, is far from an exhaustive one. Dialect continues to collect on our doorstep.

What success has attended this effort is due to the wide and discerning interest of our correspondents, who have shown real pride in making our collection as complete and authenic as humanly possible. I wish to express to all of them my gratitude for the able support they have given and are giving to this undertaking. Cordial thanks are likewise due to the newspapers mentioned above for making this experiment possible.

Since one word is sent in by more than a dozen correspondents, it has not seemed feasible to mention the names of correspondents in connection with their contributions. They are mentioned, therefore, only occasionally in connection with a theory of derivation and the like. It seems only fair to say in conclusion that Dr. John Bennett has been the real inspiration of this project, as all will realize who have followed our news articles.

Correspondents

Col. Robert W. Achurch
The Citadel
Charleston, S. C.

Dr. John Bennett
37 Legare St.
Charleston, S. C.

Mrs. Mary Hay Stroman All
2832 Heyward Street
Columbia, S. C.

Mrs. L. J. Bentz
933 Brandon St.
Columbia, S. C.

Dr. W. W. Ball
The News and Courier
Charleston, S. C.

Miss Anna Rena Blake
English Department
Lander College
Greenwood, S. C.

Mr. George B. Beach
Abbeville, S. C.

Mr. Addison Bostain, Jr.
Box 98
Newberry, S. C.

Miss Elizabeth S. Bearden
192 Mills St.
Spartanburg, S. C.

Mr. H. J. Brabham
1105 Hampton St.
Columbia, S. C.

Mr. Christie Benet
808 Pickens St.
Columbia, S. C.

Mr. James Arthur Britt
Moultrieville, S. C.

Miss Virginia Brodie
Ridge Springs, S. C.

Mr. James R. Cain
5 Lincoln Road
York, S. C.

Mr. J. C. Calhoun
2400 Blossom St.
Columbia, S. C.

Miss Edith Campbell
524 Cashua St.
Darlington, S. C.

Mrs. A. J. Cauthen
Orangeburg, S. C.

Mr. N. A. Chamberlain
73 Bull St.
Charleston, S. C.

Dean Arney R. Childs
University of S. C.
Columbia, S. C.

Mr. James A. Clarkson
Hopkins, S. C.

Miss Caroline S. Coleman
Fountain Inn, S. C.

Rev. Walter Y. Cooley
Great Falls, S. C.

Prof. Philip Covington
Wofford College
Spartanburg, S. C.

Mrs. J. W. Cox
Johnston, S. C.

Dr. Harold L. Creager
Lutheran Seminary
Columbia, S. C.

Mrs. Claude E. Creason
730 Belt Line Boulevard
Columbia, S. C.

Prof. Bartow Culp
Medical College
Charleston, S. C.

Dean S. M. Derrick
University of S. C.
Columbia, S. C.

Miss Laura deShields
203 Tomassee Ave.
Greenville, S. C.

Miss Louise M. Douglas
122 South Erwin St.
Darlington, S. C.

Mrs. L. J. DuBose
University Press
Columbia, S. C.

Mrs. W. L. Dunovant, Sr.
Edgefield, S. C.

Prof. T. E. Epting
Newberry College
Newberry, S. C.

English Department
% Prof. H. Morris Cox
Clemson College
Clemson, S. C.

Mr. Buist M. Fanning
Springfield, S. C.

Prof. Thomas A. FitzGerald
University of S. C.
Columbia, S. C.

Mrs. John R. Fogle
Orangeburg, S. C.

Dr. R. B. Furman
Sumter, S. C.

Miss Jeanne Gadsden
Summerville, S. C.

Mr. W. W. Gerald
Aynor, S. C.

Mr. Robert A. Gettys
Rock Hill, S. C.

Dr. J. Heyward Gibbes
1700 Green Street
Columbia, S. C.

Mr. David V. Gleaton
Springfield, S. C.

Mr. Cecil Goodson
1412 Barefoot St.
Hartsville, S. C.

Mrs. Mary Hemphill Greene
Abbeville, S. C.

Mr. B. A. Grimball
Route 1
Charleston, S. C.

Mrs. R. O'Neil Hair
Holly Hill, S. C.

Mrs. J. M. Halford
Blackville, S. C.

Dr. French Haynes
Coker College
Hartsville, S. C.

Mrs. J. R. Heller
Seneca, S. C.

Miss Ella Hendrix
Lexington, S. C.

Mr. N. B. Hicks
Timmonsville, S. C.

Mrs. Gedney M. Howe
Box 807
Charleston, S. C.

Mr. James A. Hoyt
U. S. Court of Claims
Washington, D. C.

Mrs. T. W. Irick
Vance, S. C.

Mr. Arthur L. Jones
102 E. Stone Ave.
Greenville, S. C.

Dr. Waldo H. Jones
Myrtle Beach, S. C.

Mrs. T. S. Kelley
Cades, S. C.

Mr. N. D. Lesesne
Due West, S. C.

Mr. George E. Lever
1307 Summerville Ave.
Columbia, S. C.

Mr. W. J. Ligon
Anderson, S. C.

Dr. E. C. McCants
Anderson, S. C.

Dean S. J. McCoy
Winthrop College
Rock Hill, S. C.

Mrs. W. W. McIver
111 Hibben St.
Mt. Pleasant, S. C.

Mr. C. M. McKinnon
Hartsville, S. C.

Mrs. R. L. Meriwether
1410 Devonshire Road
Columbia, S. C.

Dr. Chapman J. Milling
915 Belt Line Boulevard
Columbia, S. C.

Dean Elford C. Morgan
Converse College
Mt. Pleasant, S. C.

Prof. Claude Neuffer
University of S. C.
Columbia, S. C.

Miss Elizabeth Nickles
Erskine College
Due West, S. C.

Prof. J. E. Norwood
811 Albion Rd.
Columbia, S. C.

Dr. C. W. O'Driscoll
Medical College of S. C.
Charleston, S. C.

Office Help
% The Edisto Citizen
Springfield, S. C.

Mrs. Marion T. Oliver
Columbia, S. C.

Mrs. Courtenay Olney
43 Fenwick Drive
Windemere
Charleston, S. C.

Mrs. Hattie Padgett
Neeses, S. C.

Col. Basil Manley Parks
University of S. C.
Columbia, S. C.

Mrs. F. L. Parks
Meggett, S. C.

Mrs. Dessie Pitts
Erskine College
Due West, S. C.

Miss Ann Porcher
9 Water St.
Charleston, S. C.

Miss Dorothy Porter
St. Andrews Parish School
Box 98
St. Andrews Branch
Charleston, S. C.

Col. F. G. Potts
Mt. Pleasant, S. C.

Mrs. Leila H. Price
Wadmalaw Island, S. C.

Miss Laura Jeannette Quattlebaum
Conway, S. C.

Mr. H. S. Reaves
24 New St.
Charleston, S. C.

Mr. M. C. Riser
Cross Hill
Berkeley Co., S. C.

Mr. A. S. Salley
901 Laurens St.
Columbia, S. C.

Mr. Olin J. Salley
Salley, S. C.

Mr. Walter I. Salmonson
32 Society St.
Charleston, S. C.

Mrs. Herbert Ravenel Sass
23 Legare St.
Charleston, S. C.

Dr. & Mrs. Edward Schlaeffer
1502 Richland St.
Columbia, S. C.

Mr. Edwin G. Seibels
1332 Pickens St.
Columbia, S. C.

Dr. Milledge B. Seigler
836 Barnwell St.
Columbia, S. C.

Mr. Arthur B. Shaw
1502 Hampton St.
Columbia, S. C.

Mrs. T. R. Shuford
Anderson, S. C.

Miss Emma E. Shuler
Elloree, S. C.

Mrs. Enoch Smith
Route 4
Rosewood Drive
Columbia, S. C.

Mr. S. G. Stoney
129 X Tradd St.
Charleston, S. C.

Mrs. Jane P. Strother
10 Park Ave.
Sumter, S. C.

Dr. E. P. Vandiver, Jr.
Furman Univ.
Greenville, S. C.

Miss Lucile Vassar
Carolina Orphanage
Columbia, S. C.

Dr. Gilbert P. Voigt
1904 Harrington St.
Newberry, S. C.

Mrs. J. M. Wallace
Alcolu, S. C.

Miss Carmen Walpole
St. Andrews Parish School
Charleston, S. C.

Miss May A. Waring
2 Atlantic St.
Charleston, S. C.

Miss Mildred Werts
Newberry, S. C

Mr. Charles C. West
Box 324
Tryon, N. C.

Mrs. O. T. West
Box 533
Naval Base, S. C.

Mrs. E. W. Wilson
Wadmalaw Island, S. C.

Mrs. Hattie S. Witte
Mt. Pleasant, S. C.

Mr. L. S. Wolfe
Orangeburg, S. C.

Mr. M. A. Wright
Linville Falls, N. C.

Mrs. Leila L. Zealey
Meggett, S. C.

B. GLOSSARY

Abbreviations used

Bart.   *A Glossary of Words and Phrases*, by John Russell Bartlett, 1859.

Cf.   Compare (cites a word of similar but not identical use).

EDD   *English Dialect Dictionary*, by Joseph Wright, 1898–1905.

F. and W.   *New Standard Dictionary*, by Funk and Wagnalls, 1925.
Gonz.   *The Black Border*, by Ambrose Gonzales, 1922.
NID   Webster's *New International Dictionary*, 1950.
S. and C.   *South Carolina Bird Life*, by Alexander Sprunt, Jr., and E. Burnham Chamberlain.
Turner   *Africanisms in the Gullah Dialect*, Lorenzo Dow Turner, 1949.
Wen.   *American Dialect Dictionary*, by Harold Wentworth, 1944.

act: *v.i.* To perform on a horizontal bar; to perform on any gymnastic paraphernalia, as parallel bars, etc. Used before the days of gymnasiums. School boys made their own *acting poles*.

acting pole: *n.* An improvised horizontal bar, such as was formerly put up by school boys, and on which they *acted* during recess. Also called *acting bar, action bar*.

afeard [ə'fjɛəd]: *past part. adj.* Afraid. Illiterate. EDD.

ageable: *adj.* Advanced in years, old. Wen.

aggravate: *v.t.* To exasperate, to irritate, to provoke. NID.

agin [ə'gɪn]: *prep.* Against; towards, in the direction of. "Over *agin* the river," "I'm *agin* it." NID, Wen., *again*.

all the: in combination with adjectives and adverbs forms a superlative. "Is that *all the fast* you can go?" "Here's *all the high* we can climb." Also used with the comparative with the same effect: "This is *all the further* I can go with you." (This is the farthest I can go.) Wen., *PADS*, 6, p. 4: *all the, all the farther*.

all around: *adv.* Near. "He came *all around* winning." "He was *all around* passing out."

alligator corn: *n.* The seed pods of the water lily.

allow: *v.t.* To concede; to suppose; to assume; to say; to say with an implied threat. "We *'lowed* you wudden [wasn't] comin', so we left." "We asked Ma, and she *'lowed* we must be home by sundown." EDD, *allow*. To suppose, to consider, to be of opinion.

all two: *pron.* Both. Gullah.

alter: *v.t.* (of domestic animals) to castrate. NID, Wen.

ambeer ['æmbɛə, 'æmbjɛə]: *n.* The *amber* colored tobacco spittle.

ambition: *n.* A quick temper. Cf. Bart.

ambitious: *adj.* Hot tempered, quick tempered. Bart., Cf. Wen.

Andy-over: *n. Antony-over, anti-over.* This boy's ball game is played by two sides, one on each side of a building, such as the schoolhouse. The side in possession of the ball shouts: *Andy-over!*

to denote that the ball is in play. It is then thrown over the house, and if it is caught, the one catching it is entitled to go with his team around to the other side and throw the ball at anyone of the other team. If the ball is not caught, it must be thrown back. EDD, NID, *Antony-over*. Also: *hail-over*.

answer: *n*. A message. "Cap'n, de *answer* we git wuz come cut crossties for wunnuh. Dat de right, enti?" The message we got was to come and cut crossties for you. That is right, is it not? Gullah and coastal Negro usage.

antigodlin: *adj*. Awry, askew, irregular. "Your skirt is all *antigodlin*" (hangs unevenly). Variants are *Sarahgodlin*, *Sallygodlin*, etc. Cf. *sidegodlin*, *q.v.*

any more: *adv*. Once more, again. "I am drinking Coca-Colas *any more*." I am drinking Coca-Colas again. (I had stopped drinking them.) Cf. Bart. under *all*.

argufy, arfigy: *v.i*. To argue, with a connotation of aimlessness. NID, Wen., EDD.

ary, airy ['ærɪ]: *adj*. From *e'er a*. A, any, any at all. "Is there *ary* man here who has ever seen a ghost?" Wen.

as: *conj*. Than. "I'd rather do this *as* that."

askeared: *adj*. Same as *afeard*.

attitude: *n*. Direction. "Boss, I bu'n off one side de road lak you beena tell me, an' I gwi' bu'n off turrer side fus time I ketch de win' in de right *attitude*." Negro usage.

aunty, aunt: *n*. A title given to elderly Negro women in the upcountry. If the name follows the title the form *aunt* is used: "*Aunt* Dinah." NID, Wen., EDD.

back: *v.t*. To write an address on, as a letter. NID, Wen., EDD.

back water: *v.i*. To retreat; to withdraw from a position, attitude, or opinion. Bart.

bait: *n*. All that one can eat. A *bait* of plums, watermelon, oysters, etc. Cf. NID, *bait*, n. 3, a; EDD.

baker ['bæ:kə, 'bækə, 'bækɪ]: *n*. Tobacco. "I was so skeerd I swallowed my *baker*." Cf. Wen., *'baccer*, etc.; EDD, *backy*.

balcony: *n*. A small side porch with an iron railing, usually ornate. Charleston.

banter: *v.t*. To make an offer to buy. "He *bantered* me for the hog."

barrow ['barə]: *n*. A male hog, castrated, EDD, *barrow*, sb. 1, NID.

basket name: *n.* A pet name given by Negro nurses to their helpless infant charges. Used before the rites of christening, lest some evil spirit, hearing the true name before it is ritually bound to the child, should call the child's spirit from the body and enter into the child, thus making it a changeling. They also give basket names to their own children, which sometimes usurp the place of the real name, which is thus completely lost.

bateau: *n.* A small river boat with a flat bottom, curved slightly upward lengthwise. NID. Also called *trus'-me-God bateau.* Charleston and environs.

batra ['bætrə]: *v.t.* To beat clothes on a wooden block in washing them. St. John's Parish, Berkeley. Cf. *battling stick,* the stick with which one stirs the clothes in the boiling wash pot. Georgia.

battle: *v.t.* To beat, as clothes, with a *battling stick* in washing them. Same as *batra.*

batten: *v.t.* To beat clothes in the process of washing them. This is done with a *battlin' stick.* Central S. C. Same as *batra,* Berkeley.

battling stick: *n.* A stick with which clothes are stirred while boiling in the pot, and are beaten in the process of washing.

bat wing: *n.* See *old hog.*

bay: *n.* A low place or depression, whether containing water or not, and usually covered with undergrowth or thicket. Cf. NID, *bay,* n. 3.

bear: *n.* In the phrase: "The *bear* got him," he was overcome by the heat, had a sunstroke. Cf. *monkey.*

beast: *n.* An uncastrated domestic animal, as a bull, boar, or stallion. Wen., *beast,* 2.

beat the straws: *phr.* To reinforce the rhythm of a tune being played on a violin, by beating with straws on the strings at the time that the violinist draws the bow across them. This is done by holding one straw in each hand between the forefinger and the middle finger and striking the violin strings in the space between the bow and the fingers of the violinist. Obsolete?

belong: *v.i.* To be supposed, to be expected; to be demanded by custom. "If a drink *belongs* to be hot, I want it hot." "John *belongs* to be in the tenth grade, but he was out a year." "You really *belong* to go with us." Wen.; EDD, *belong,* 4, to be accustomed, to be in the habit of; to be one's duty, to behoove.

bias: *adj.* At an acute angle. In the expression *bias road,* a road leading off at an acute angle from the main road. Berkeley County and Williamsburg County.

big: *v.t.* To make pregnant. Wen., EDD, *big*, adj. 2.

big blue darter: *n.* Cooper's hawk. S. and C.

big dog: *n.* A bigwig, "big bug." Bart.

big eye: *n.* A child is said to have a *big eye* when he helps himself to more food than he can eat. Also applied to older persons. "His eye is bigger than his belly," is an often-heard expression of the same idea. *Big eye* expresses also greed in general. "He got de *big eye*," he wants more than his share.

big-hominy: *n.* Hulled corn. Also called *lye hominy*.

big indigo: *n.* Eastern blue grosbeak. S. and C.

big meeting: *n.* A protracted series of revival meetings, often with two services a day and picnic dinner on the grounds; also one day of such double services. Bart.

biggity: *adj.* Impertinent, insolent, bumptious. Wen. EDD, *big-otty, bigety*.

biled shirt: *n.* A stiff-bosomed dress shirt, a *boiled shirt*. For the pronunciation, cf. *pint* for *point, jint* for *joint, kwile* for *coil*, etc., Wen., *bile*, 2.

bird-battling: *n.* Bat-fowling; beating the bushes or trees where birds are roosting at night, dazzling them with lights, and striking them down with sticks or brushes. Cf. NID. Also: *bird-thrashing, bird-blinding, bird-framming*, Cf. EDD, *batfolding, batfoul, birdbatting*.

bittle, vittle, wittle: *n. Victuals*, food. Gullah.

blackberry winter: *n.* A late cold spell, a spell of cold weather late in the spring. Seneca, Union County. Wen. Cf. EDD, *blackberry summer*.

black bottle: *n.* Poison. To give one the *black bottle* was supposed to have been a method of getting rid of a patient in a hospital. Charleston.

black frost: *n.* A freeze, forming ice, but without hoar frost. EDD. Cf. NID. Plantation people felt safe to return from summer resorts after the first *black frost*.

Black Moke: *n.* "A Negro having the clear, coal-black hue of the African tribe of Mocoes from the valley of the Congo." John Bennett.

blate: *v.i.* To bleat. An upcountry pronunciation. Cf. NID under *blatant*. Wen.

blaze-faced: *adj.* Of a horse or cow, having a blaze, or white stripe running down the face; also, of a cow, having the entire head white.

blink: *n.* Milk that has turned or begun to turn sour. Wen.; EDD, *blink,* v. II, 8.

blinky: *adj.* Of milk, turning sour: Wen., NID.

blood and 'ounds, blooden hound: *excl.* and *n.* 1. A clipped eighteenth-century oath: "By the blood and wounds of the crucified Saviour!" Modified by deference to Puritan opinion. 2. A bullfrog. Onomatopeia.

bluebelly: *n.* 1. A proud, pretentious person. Term of reproach. 2. A Yankee soldier during Reconstruction.

bluegum, bluegummed: *adj.* Having a disease of the gums which causes them to appear blue at the edges next to the teeth. Said to be caused by pyorrhea. Observed only in Negroes. In popular superstition the bite of a bluegummed person is poisonous. Dr. Chapman Milling questions the connection with pyorrhea, since bluegummed Negroes have been observed with perfectly sound teeth. Samuel G. Stoney suggests: "Possibly caused by partial pigmentation of the gums of black Negroes."

blue nose: *n.* An overstrict Sabbatarian.

bluejohn: *n.* 1. Skimmed milk. 2. Same as *blink.* So called from the color of skimmed milk. EDD, *blue,* adj. 3.

blue peter: *n.* The American coot. S. and C.

blue yellow-backed warbler: *n.* The southern parula warbler. S. and C.

board: *n.* A shake, a quarter to a half inch in thickness, from four to five inches wide and three to four feet long, split from an oak block (not sawed), and used for roofing barns, sheds, and other outhouses. Bart.

board: *v.t.* To beat with a *board.* Only of persons.

bodock: *n.* The *bois-d'arc* or Osage orange. Sporadic and obsolescent in S. C.

boer dollar: *n.* A silver dollar, carried as a lucky piece. Said to have originated among British soldiers during the *Boer* War.

bofe: *adj.* Both. Prevailingly but not exclusively a Negro usage.

bog [bɔg, bag]: *n.* Rice cooked with poultry or game; pilau. Usually only in compounds: *chicken bog, squirrel bog.*

bogue: *v.i.* To trudge slowly. Usually with adv. *along.* Cf. Wen. Obsolescent, Aiken County.

booger[1] ['buɡə]: *n.* Rheum dried and caked in the nostrils. Children's speech: "Mama says you mustn't pick *boogers* out of your nose with your fingers; you must use your handkerchief." *V.i.* see *PADS*, 13, p. 16.

booger[2] ['buɡə]: *n.* 1. A head louse. 2. A mischievous child. 3. A ghost or goblin. "Playing ghosts and *boogers.*"—Eudora Welty, *The Golden Apples*, p. 10. Cf. *boogerman.* EDD, *bugger*, a hobgoblin, puck, ghost.

boogerman ['buɡə‚mæn]: *n.* A bugbear, bugaboo; the devil. NID, Wen.

bootleg: *n.* A twenty-four pound sack of flour. Dutch Fork. Possibly so called because of its shape.

bossman: *n.* 1. An employer. 2. An overseer in charge of labor. Cf. NID, *boss*, n. 1.

boughten: *past part.* Bought, as contrasted with homemade. Also *store boughten.* EDD, *boughten.*

bowdacious: *adj.* 1. Extreme, unrestrained, outrageous, bold, impudent. Var. *bardacious bodacious.* "*Bowdacious* behavior." 2. Unruly. "You *bardacious* little hussy!"

bowdaciously: *adv.* Thoroughly. "If you don't behave yourself I'll wear you *bowdaciously* out."

box: *n.* A tin or can with its contents. "A *box* of salmon." Dutch Fork. "Fish *box*," a can of salmon, etc. Santee.

box-ankled: *adj.* Having a conformation of legs and feet so that in walking the ankle bones are supposed to strike together. Often used in vituperation, *e.g.*: "You freckle-faced, knock-kneed, *box-ankled* son of a gun."

box cooter: *n.* 1. The box tortoise. 2. A close-mouthed, uncommunicative person.

bramboo briar: *n.* The *bamboo* briar.

brass-ankle: *n.* 1. A person of mixed ancestry (Negro, Indian, white). 2. A Croatan. Derogatory and insulting. "Said to refer to *brass anklets* worn by Indians to distinguish them from Negroes." L. J. DuBose.

break-down: *n.* A country dancing party. Cf. Bart.: A riotous dance. Also called *hoe-down.*

breast-child: *n.* An unweaned infant.

breddah ['brɛdə]: *n. pl.* Brothers, *brethren.* Gonz.: *Bredduh.*

briarpatch chillun: *n. pl.* Illegitimate children. See *ditch edge, long-o'-de-paat, woods colt*, etc.

brimsy ['brɪmzɪ]: *adj.* Variant of *brinjin'*.

brinjer ['brɪndʒə]: *n.* Extremely cold weather. "How's the weather outside, Uncle Ned?" "'E *brinjer!*" Rare except in coastal area of S. C., Rock Hill, Aiken.

brinjin' ['brɪndʒɪn]: *adv.* Extremely (cold). "It's *brinjin'* cold today." Sporadic and obsolescent in S. C. except on coast.

broadleaf tree: *n.* The magnolia grandifolia.

broke-bone fever, broken-bone fever: *n.* Dengue fever. Bart.: *break-bone* fever.

brotus, broatus, broadus ['brɔtəs, 'brɔdəs]: *n.* An extra handful in a measure, an additional one or more to a purchased dozen, given by hucksters, street peddlers and market-women. Cf. "lagniappe" of New Orleans. Charleston and coastal S. C. Origin undetermined. EDD, *brotta*, "a few drops, a small quantity, a little in addition" offers a possibility.

brown: *n.* A cent piece. Charleston. NID. Also: *red.* General.

brown: *adv.* Well, excellently, suitably. "Done up *brown.*" Applies to all sorts of activities. Borrowed from the kitchen.

brownie: *n.* A cent piece. Wen.

brung: *past part.* Brought. Illiterate. Wen.

brute: *n.* Same as *beast.*

bubbies: *n. pl.* The female breasts.

bucket mixture, bucket candy: *n.* An assortment of small candy consisting of gumdrops, lozenges, bonbons of various flavors, etc., purveyed in and sold from a large bucket.

buckra ['bʌkrə]: *n.* White man. Negro dialect of coastal and lower S. C. *Poor buckra;* 1. A white man who owned no slaves. Contemptuous. Obsolete. 2. A poor white man. Turner, p. 191.

bullace, bullis ['bʊlɪs], **bullison** (Pendleton): *n.* The bullace grape. Wen.; EDD, *bullace*, a wild plum.

bullbat: *n.* The Florida nighthawk, S. and C.; the common leather-winged bat.

bullet hawk: *n.* The marsh hawk. Probably so called because of the *bullet-like* dart made upon his prey. S. and C. Cf. NID.

bullfinch: *n.* The green-tailed towhee. S. and C. Cf. NID.

bullyrag: *v.t.* To bully. NID, Wen., EDD.

bumbee: *n.* The bumblebee. A Scottish usage surviving in lower S. C. NID, EDD.

bumblebee coot: *n.* The ruddy duck. NID, S. and C.

bumbye: *adv.* Bye and bye. Negro usage.

bumfidgets: *n. pl.* An aggravated state of nervousness; fidgets. "Children, stop that noise; it gives me the *bumfidgets.*"

bumfuzzle: *v.t.* To confuse, to fuddle, to puzzle, to perplex.

bumfuzzled: *adj. part.* Confused, fuddled, puzzled.

burnt-tail Jinny: *n.* The will-o'-the-wisp. The feminine mate or counterpart of Jack-o'-Lantern.

burrhead: *n.* 1. A Negro. General. 2. Any illiterate or incompetent person. Conway.

butterball: *n.* The ruddy duck. NID, S. and C.

butterbean: *n.* Sieva bean; lima bean. Upper S. C. In the lower and coastal area these are called *sivvy* beans. Wen., NID.

butts: *n. pl.* Chunks of pork, mostly fat, trimmed from other pieces, as hams, and salt cured. Cf. NID, *butt*, n. 1, a. Also *butt meat.*

buzzard: *n.* A term of reproach, applied to a person of disreputable character and reputation. NID.

buzzard-blow-'e-nose: *n.* The stinkhorn.

buzzard bread: *n.* The seed balls of the plane tree, also called sycamore.

cactified: *adj.* Assuming a false appearance of superiority, "stuck-up." Upcountry S. C.

calico-back: *n.* The ruddy turnstone. NID, S. and C.

callihootin [ˌkælɪ'hutn̩], **cahootin', gallihootin:** *adv.* At high speed, same as "lickety-split."

candy: *n.* Stick candy as opposed to bonbons or French candy.

can't see: *n.* The period of darkness before day and after dark. "He worked from *can't see* to *can't see*," from before day until after dark.

cascade: *v.i.* Euphemism for vomit. Charleston Negro usage.

case, casing: *n.* The smaller or larger intestine of hogs used for stuffing sausage, scrapple, etc.

cat owl: *n.* The great horned owl.

catawampus, caliwampus, kittywampus [ˌkætə'wɔmpəs, ˌkætɪ-]: *adj.* Awry, askew, not fitting properly in place. NID.

cat squirrel: *n.* The gray squirrel. NID.

catticornered, catacornered, cattibias, catabias, cattiwampus, catawampus ['kætɪˌkɔnəd, 'kætə-, ˌkætɪ'baɪəs, 'katə'baɪəs]: *adj.* and *adv.* Askew, awry, diagonal, diagonally. Wen.

cayless-pin: *n. Careless* pin. A straight pin as distinguished from a safety, or *careful* pin. Negro, coastal area.

chair road: *n.* A private or community road for litters only, not wide enough for vehicles. Obsolete.

character. *n.* An unscrupulous, unreliable, untrustworthy person; an amusing person; an extreme individualist. *Character*, in various meanings, is sometimes heard with the accent on second syllable.

cham-chack: *n.* The red-bellied woodpecker. S. and C.

chaneyberry ['tʃɛnɪˌbɛrɪ]: *n.* A widespread pronunciation of *chinaberry*. EDD under *cheeny*. *Chaney* is a dialect pronunciation of *China*. Wen., *chany*.

chaney briar: *n.* The China briar, the *bramboo briar*, smilax.

change: *v.t.* Same as *alter.* "Git a bull an' *change* um for a ox." Charleston.

Charleston buzzard, Charleston eagle: *n.* The black vulture. S. and C.

chaw: *n.* A quid of tobacco. NID, Wen., EDD.

chaw: *v.t.* To chew, NID, Wen.; EDD, *chaw up*, to defeat.

chawed: *past part., adj.* Defeated, beaten. In a literal or figurative sense.

chay-chay: *n.* The blue-gray gnatcatcher. S. and C.

cheweeka [tʃɪ'wikə]: *n.* 1. The killdeer. S. and C. 2. An insignificant, puny person. "You little *cheweeka!*" Coastal area.

chicken-flesh: *n.* Goose-flesh. Union County. EDD.

chicken guts: *n.* A child's name for the symbol &.

chicken hawk: *n.* Florida red-shouldered hawk; northern red-shouldered hawk. S. and C. Cf. NID.

childer ['tʃɪldə]: *n.* Children. Obsolescent.

chimney sweep: *n.* The chimney swift.

chinchy: *adj.* Stingy. Wen.

chips and whetstones: *n. pl.* Small amounts; small partial payments. "He pays his account in *chips and whetstones.*"

chitlings, chittlings: *n. pl.* Chitterlings.

choptongued: *adj.* Descriptive of a dog with a short yelp instead of a full round, bell-like voice, when warm on the trail.

Christmas-give, -gift, -giff: *n.* A greeting on Christmas morning. The person who says this first is supposed to receive a present. "I caught him *Christmas-give,*" I said *Christmas-give* to him before he said it to me. "I done caught you *Christmas-give.* What you gwi' gimme?"

chuff [tʃʌf]: *adj.* See *grum.* NID; EDD, *chuff*, adj., ill-tempered, etc.

chuffle-jawed: *adj.* Same as *whampsy-jawed.*

chunk: *v.t.* 1. To throw, as a missile: *"Chunk* a rock at that snake."* Lower and coastal S. C. 2. To prod. *"Chunk* the fire before it goes out."* NID, Wen., Bart. Dr. Chapman Milling suggests the Indian game *chunga* as the origin of *chunk.*

chunk: *n.* A piece of indeterminate size and shape, as of coal, ice, wood. NID.

civey cat: *n.* The polecat. From *civet* cat.

claphat: *adj.* Hasty, reckless. A woman hasty in speech and deed is frequently referred to as "that *claphat* wench," as one who claps on her hat and goes in haste. Derogatory.

[1]**clay-eater, chalk-eater**: *n.* One who eats clay, especially a kind of clay found in Aiken, Calhoun, Greenwood, and probably other counties. Said to cause a bluish complexion. Addicts moving away

[1] The *Encyclopedia Americana* says under *geophagy:* "The practice of eating some kind of earthy matter as clay or chalk, common among uncivilized people, such as the South American Ottamacs, the Indians of the Hudson Bay country, the West Indian Blacks, the Negroes in some of the United States and among the less civilized whites in the mountain districts of Tennessee and Kentucky. In some cases it is probably used to allay hunger, but it is also practiced where the supply of food is sufficient. Among chlorotic young women a similarly depraved appetite is not uncommon. It is likely to terminate fatally in dropsy or dysentery." Correspondents report that a distended stomach is one of the marked symptoms.

Dr. Chapman Milling suggests that the practice of geophagy may be an instinctive attempt to supply a calcium deficiency "since children with a calcium deficiency have been observed to nibble chalk in school."

Another surmise is that clay eaters suffer from hookworms and that clay eating is an instinctive counter measure to scour the hookworms out of the infested intestines. This surmise was advanced about forty years ago when the movement to eradicate the hookworm disease was strongest.

The practice of clay eating still persists. Addicts will sometimes carry their clay in a paper bag to work. Asked what the clay tastes like, they say: "You know the earth smell when a shower of rain comes up on the dry ground? That's how it tastes." White clay is preferred if available, but red is also used.

Doctors treat geophagia by substituting block magnesia for the clay, thus satisfying the taste without harm to the system.

from the source of supply have it shipped to them. In default of clay they eat starch or chalk. NID, Wen., Bart.

clever ['klɛvə]: *adj.* Kind, obliging; good-natured. NID, Wen, EDD.

clod buster: *n.* A fairly heavy rain. Hill country. Also: *Litered knot floater.* Peedee.

clout: *n.* A quilted pad used to protect the outer clothes of infants, a pilch, Cf. NID, Wen.

clum, clumb: *past tense* and *past part.* of *climb.* NID, Wen., EDD.

coal-burner: *n.* Applied by Negroes to a preacher who is up to the minute and pleasing in every way. A complimentary title. Obsolescent. This word arose at the time when the *coal burning* locomotives, superior to the older wood-burners, were introduced.

coat: *n.* Petticoat. "Missy, yo' *coat* duh heng." Your slip is showing. Negro usage of Charleston. EDD.

cock-eyed: *adj.* 1. Describing a form of strabismus in which the visual axes diverge; wall-eyed. Opposite of cross-eyed. 2. Awry, askew. "Your plan is all *cock-eyed.*" (Slang). A favorite expletive: "I'll tell the *cock-eyed* world . . . ." NID, EDD.

colcock ['kolkak], **coolcock:** *v.t.* To knock out, knock cold, with a connotation of knocking with a blunt instrument on the side or back of the head. Origin undetermined.

come fresh: *v.i.* Of cows: to freshen.

come-hither shovel: *n.* A shovel reshaped so that the blade is at a right angle with the handle, used like a hoe for digging in pluff mud and marshes, for clams, etc.

come sick: *v.i.* To menstruate.

come through: *v.i.* 1. To pass through a religious experience at a revival meeting, after one has "got religion," is converted. Negro usage. 2. Of epileptics: to recover from an attack.

common: *adj.* Friendly, sociable, not distant, dignified or reserved. "I lack Mr. Snowden, he so *common!*" Highly complimentary. NID, *common*, adj. 3.b.

conjure ['kʌndʒə] **ball:** *n.* A ball made of such weird objects as dead lizards and bats, frog's legs, snake skins dried and tied together. The ball is then thrown under the front steps of the victim, who finds it and is conjured thereby. As a result he knows himself to be exposed to the visitation of sperrits and hants, to be ridden at night by witches. The *conjure ball* has proved quite effective with the superstitious, causing hysterics and even death. Obsolescent, but probably not obsolete.

cooglerism ['kuglərɪzm̩]: *n.* Mediocre verse, written seriously, but taken by the public with a smile. Columbia and Richland County. The late J. Gordon Coogler ['kuglə] was a poetaster of Columbia, S. C. His most quoted lines (here cited from memory) are.

> Alas for the South, her books are few;
> She is not given to literature.

When his attention was called to the imperfect rhyme, he wrote:

> Alas for the South, her books grow fewer;
> She is not given to literature.

cool-doo: *n.* The wood ibis. Negro usage of the Pee-Dee. Probably a corruption of *curlew.*

cooling board: *n.* A board or table on which the dead are laid out.

coon-song: *n.* Any secular Negro song, in contrast to spirituals. When one gets converted, one is expected to refrain from singing reels and *coon-songs.* Obsolescent.

cooter ['kutə, 'kʊtə]: *n.* The box tortoise; the fresh-water turtle. Lower S. C.

cooter-backed: *adj.* Highly arched, as the back of a cooter. Applied especially to dirt roads which are so constructed as to shed the rainfall and thus to prevent water from standing in the driveway and puddling the road.

cooter grass: *n.* 1. Portulaca or purslane, gathered by children as food for small captive tortoises, the succulent stems and leaves being considered choice for that purpose. 2. The water-shield, a plant kin to the water-lily, growing in ponds and sluggish streams. NID.

cooter log: *n.* Any log or bench used as a seat for chronic idlers and loafers. The *cooter* is well known for crawling out of the water on a log and lying by the hour without moving. Coastal region. Cf. NID, *cooter,* v.i.

cop: *v.t.* To obtain by ability, alertness or shrewdness: "She *copped* the first prize." To gain by quickness. "He *copped* the first place in line." To snatch, with a connotation of stealth. "Let's *cop* a watermelon on the way." NID, *cop,* v.t. 1; EDD, *cop,* 4.v.1.

corn dodger: *n.* 1. A lump of cornmeal dough, flavored with onions and black or red pepper, dropped into a pot of greens and boiled for half an hour, Also called *corn dumpling*. 2. A cake of baked corn bread. Wen. Cf. EDD, *dad*, a large piece, a lump, a portion; *dodge*, a large cut or slice of food; a small lump of something moist and thick; *dodgel*, a large piece or lump.

corn dumpling: *n.* Same as *corn dodger*, 1, except that it is also cooked in the stock of cured boiled ham or shoulder. NID, *corn dodger*. 2.

corn-field lawyer: *n.* Same as *yard-axe lawyer*, *q.v.*

cornfield Negro: *n.* In slavery days, a Negro who was suitable only for work in the field; the same general meaning obtains today.

corn shucking: *n.* A social gathering for shucking corn and merrymaking, usually with refreshment. *Husking* is not usually heard. NID, Wen.

corporosity: *n.* The body, the physical man. Used in a familiar and jocular sense. See *segaciate*.

cotton field watermelon: *n.* See *cymlin'*.

country fever: *n.* Malaria.

cowcumber: *n.* Cucumber. NID, EDD, Wen.

cream glands: *n. pl.* The highly prized thymus glands of calves and lambs. Also called *sweetbreads*.

creed: *n.* In the expression: "my creed," a term of endearment. Gaelic: *mo cridhe*, my heart. John Bennett.

creek boy [krik]: *n.* A boy employed to bring in crabs and other sea food from the creeks of the coastal area to boarding houses, hotels, etc.

creen: *v.i.* To lean away from the vertical position, said of houses, barns, etc., whose walls were not properly braced in building. Cf. NID, *careen*, and *PADS*, 13, p. 17.

crick: *n.* A salt water inlet; a creek.

crickboy: *n.* Same as *creek boy*, low country pronunciation.

cripple: *n.* Scrapple. Orangeburg. Origin undetermined.

critter: *n.* A creature, especially a domestic animal; in some localities applied only to a horse. Sometimes pronounced *creeter*. Also applied to persons in a patronizing and commiserating sense: "old *critter*," "poor *critter*," "poor old *critter*."

[2]crocus-sack, croker-sack: *n.* Coarse sack made of jute fiber or hemp. NID, Wen.

[2] "Suggested possible origin: The croaker's sack of the ship surgeon into which dismembered portions of wounded men were dumped, ...

Wonderful!

crome: *v.t.* To overpower, to subdue.

crowbill: *n.* The American coot. S. and C.

crud (krʌd): *n.* Filth.

crummy: *adj.* Worthless, inferior. Like a *crumb*, in being worthless, insignificant.

crut: *n.* A term of endearment. A father says to his wife or daughter: "My little *crut*." Maybe connected with EDD, *crut* a dwarf; a boy or girl stunted in growth.

crutty ['krʌtɪ]: *adj.* Very dirty, so that the dirt almost forms a crust. *Crut* is the shaggy, rough part of oak bark, and may be the origin of this word. One is tempted also to think of French *crotté*, and *crud*.

cubbage ['kʌbɪdʒ]: *adj.* Small. *Cubbage pot*, a small pot, the idea being that it will hold only enough food for one person. May be related to *cubby*.

cubbage hole: *n.* The depression in the middle of the back of the neck at the base of the skull. May be from *cubby hole*.

cuckatoo owl: *n.* The great horned owl, so called in imitation of its hoot(?).

cuffey ['kʌfɪ]: *n.* A Negro. Patronizing, sometimes with a shade of derision, but lacking the contempt of *po' buckra* used by the Negroes in the lower part of the state for poor whites, or the expression *po' white* trash of the upcountry. Obsolete. *Cuffeytown* Creek is in McCormick County. Greenwood, Abbeville, Edgefield, Charleston counties. NID, Wen., Bart.

cullah-cullah ['kʌlə-'kʌlə]: *n.* The wild duck. "Gen. Alexander listed this word as American Indian." John Bennett.

curley flowers: *n. pl.* The cauliflower; survival of an English usage. EDD.

curtsey: *n.* A low bow in salutation, as practiced by slaves.

cush [kʊʃ]: *n.* Cornbread and gravy mashed up together; fried scrapple; corn meal fried with meat or oysters. There are various other recipes for cush, always involving a mixture. West African? *Kusha*, a thin cake made from ground nuts. Turner, p. 118. NID, Wen.

---

for tossing overboard after a battle, to *croak*, in London slang, meaning to die, and the surgeon, or ship's doctor being known as the *croaker*." John Bennett.

EDD also gives *croaker*, a corpse, and *croak*, to kill.

cut down: *past part., adj.* Vexed, troubled or disconcerted by some disagreeable occurrence.

cut down: *v.t.* To humble; to deflate one's egotism. NID.

cutsie, kutsie ['kʌtsɪ]: *n.* A twinge in the throat caused by swallowing something sour. Supposed to be a symptom of mumps. Origin undetermined.

cymbi: *n.* A naiad or water sprite haunting springs. Not a ghost. "The Cymbi of Eutaw Springs was once much dreaded by superstitious Negro servants; so much so that no girl or woman would go alone to the spring for water."

cymlin', cymling, simlin ['sɪmlɪn, 'sɪmlɪŋ]: *n.* 1. A small dwarf watermelon often found in cotton fields. Also called a *cotton field watermelon*. 2. A variety of a squash, the pan squash. Cf. NID, *cymling.*

daddy: *n.* The name given to elderly Negro men by the children of the family with which they were connected. Low country. Obsolescent. In the upcountry this title was *uncle*. Cf. Wen.

dah [dɑ]: *n.* A Negro nurse. Charleston and coastal S. C. "English children in India call their nurses '*Dah*'." Salmonson.

dam: *n.* A bank of spoil from a drainage or line ditch. Coastal area.

dash: *v.t.* To cast off, to reject, to relinquish, as a bad habit. Followed by prep. *away*. "Before I were converted I curse and play the fiddle. But when the grace of God were shed on my erring heart I *dash 'em away*."

day-clean: *n.* Broad daylight, sunrise, as opposed to daybreak, dawn.

day-day: *n.* A childish or lightly affectionate goodbye. Portuguese *adeos*, universally used on the west coast of Africa, God be with you! Bennett. To shake *day-day*, is to wave the hand in farewell.

dead man: *n.* The lungs or gills of a crab, not edible. Usually in the plural; supposed by Negroes to be very poisonous. EDD.

dead soldier: *n.* A bottle of beer, wine or liquor after it has been emptied. Cf. NID, *dead man;* EDD, *dead head.*

death owl: *n.* The screech owl. Cf. Shak., *Rich. III*, IV, iv, 1. 509; *Midsummer Night's Dream*, V,i, 1. 383. EDD: "It (the hooting of the screech-owl) is held to be a sure sign of death."

deep pie: *n.* Same as *pot pie.*

dem: *pron.* See *those.*

demry: *n.* A baked sweet potato. Gullah.

devil's dung: *n.* Asafetida. EDD.

devil's horse: *n.* The praying mantis. Same as *Johnny cock-horse,* etc., NID.

dicky: *n.* The ruddy duck. S. and C.

dicty: *adj.* Proud, haughty. Urban Negroes apply this term to bright mulattoes who try to pass for white. *Dictatorial* is a suggested origin.

diddle: *v.t.* To cheat, overreach, swindle. NID, EDD.

differ: *n.* 1. A quarrel. "What's the *differ?*" "Ain't no *differ.* We jus' arguin'." 2. Difference. "I don't allow no rabbit huntin' on my land." "I'm huntin' pattidges." "No *differ* what, rabbits or pattidges." EDD, *differ,* difference.

dillberries: *n.* The small lumps of excrement clingling to wool on the hindquarters of sheep at certain seasons. EDD, *dilberries.*

Dimery: *n.* A Croatan.

dirtdobber ['dɜɪt͵dabə], **-dauber:** *n.* A muddauber wasp. NID.

dis, dat, dem, de, etc. Illiterate usage for *this, that, them, the,* etc.

disfurnish [dɪsˈfʌːnɪʃ]: *v. refl.* To deprive. "I'd like to get some of your seed corn, but I don't want you to *disfurnish* yourself."

disremember: *v.t.* To forget. NID, Bart., EDD.

ditch-edge chillun: *n. pl.* Illegitimate children. Cf. *long-a-depaat chillun,* etc.

dodgers: *n.* Same as *corn dumplings.* Cf. *corn dodgers* for source.

dodratted, dodrotted [͵dadˈrætɪd, ͵dadˈratɪd]: *expl.* Same as *dratted, q.v.*

dog run: *n.* See *Georgia cabin.*

dog trot: *n.* See *Georgia cabin.*

done-tass Nigger: *n.* 1. A Negro who is worn out, aged, no longer able to do a day's work, or task. 2. A care-free Negro, happy because his task is done. From *task, n., q.v.*

doodle, doodle bug: *n.* The larval ant lion. Children are wont to shout over the conical pit of the ant lion: "*Doodle, doodle,* house afire!" When he cautiously appears, they order him back with: "Hack, *doodle,* hack!" The backward, crablike movement of the insect gives rise to the verb to *doodle,* to back out of an agreement. "*Doodle, doodle,* your house is on fire! Come get some bread and butter." Conway, M. A. Wright. The call to the doodle varies widely.

doodle: *v.i.* To back off from a position, to back out of an agreement. "I don't crawfish, and neither do I *doodle.*" See *doodle, n.*

doughboy: *n.* A conjuring puppet figure of biscuit dough, made to represent the object of one's resentment, baked, and stood so near the fire as to scorch and char to a cinder, or ruthlessly broken, thus supposedly inflicting severe pain and perhaps death on the victim of this sorcery. Cf. the ancient wax figure of witchcraft. The doughboy was sometimes broken to bits and fed to the chickens, thus insuring the humiliation and destruction of a rival in love., etc.

dough face: *n.* A false face. *Dough* may have been used originally in forming these fantastic masks.

Doughsticks: *n.* A familiar humorous nickname. Odd survival of a supposedly humorous book of one hundred years ago: "The Life and Adventures of T. Q. Philander *Doughsticks* and His Brother Damfool." Cf. *stick-in-the-mud.*

drag: *n.* A draw on a pipe, cigar, or cigarette.

drag: *v.t.* To rally, to tease. NID, Wen.

dragons: *n. pl.* Old shoes. Possibly from such shoes being worn through at the toe, and thus gaping like a *dragon.*

drap: *n.* A drop. NID, Wen.

drap: *v.i.* and *v.t.* To drop. NID, Wen.

dratted, drotted: Expletive expressing displeasure, disapproval. Applied to persons or things. Prov. English *drat,* v.t. From *God rot,* an oath. NID.

drean [-dri:n]: *v.t.* and *v.i.* To *drain,* as dishes, after rinsing. Wen.

drift: *v.i.* To walk, wander aimlessly: "We *drifted* across the field."

droll: *adj.* Uncanny, terrifying; e.g., a reported case of a deceased uncle calling on the family in his grave clothes, was described as *droll.*

drop button: *n.* A person mentally lacking, one who "ain't so right," "kind of cracky." Mt. Pleasant. A *drop button* is supposed to walk about looking around as if he had lost a button.

druce: *v.t.* To introduce. Gullah. "Ain't hunnah gwine to de chu'ch to *druce* yuh new bruddah?"

druthers ['drʌðəz]: *n. pl.* Same as *ruthers*, *q.v.* Arising from the combination of *would* and *ruther*. "I *would ruther* . . ." becoming "I *druther* . . ."

dry grins: *n. pl.* A forced or embarrassed grin, caused by teasing or rallying when one has no ready answer or defense. "When we asked him if he was going to see his girl, he had the *dry grins*." Wen. *dry grin.*

dumbbull: *n.* Same as *squeedunk*. The roaring noise reminds one of the bellowing of a *bull*.

dunghill: *adj.* Common, mongrel, of mixed breed, as: "*dunghill* hen" a common hen as distinguished from the purebred variety. Cf. EDD *dunghill bred, low-bred, low-born.*

dust settler: *n.* A light rain, sufficient only to settle the dust. (Hill country).

Dutch Fork: *n.* Place-name. Region in the fork of the Broad and Saluda rivers, so called because settled by the Germans.

Dutch whippoorwill: *n.* The chuck-will's-widow.

eat: *v.i.* To taste, as: "This ham *eats* good." Also: "This food *eats* where you hold it," tastes good. From the military use: "The gun shoots where you hold it." EDD.

ebo-colored ['ibo-'kʌləd]: *adj.* The dull, ashy black of the *Ibo* Negroes from the malarial region about the mouth of the Niger.

end: *n.* A short distance. "How far is it to the bridge?" "Not far, just a little *end*."

enduring: *adj.* Total, entire, whole. Only of time. "The *enduring* evening." Often with *whole*: "the *whole enduring* day." Wen.

enduring of: *prep.* During. NID, Wen. "He come in *endurin' of* the singing'."

enti ['ɛntɪ]: *v.*, *neg.*, and *pron.* "Is it not," "do we not," etc. in repetition of a statement in the interrogative form for confirmation. Cf. Ger. *nicht wahr?* Fr. *n'est-ce pas?* etc. The English language is in need of *enti* for our convenience. Gonz.

eye-ball: *v.t.* To stare at, to glare at. Negro: "Look here, nigger, don't you *eyeball* me." ". . . standin' outside dis window *eyeballin'* dat doll all day." Amos and Andy radio program, December 25, 1949.

fall off: *v.i.* To lose weight. There is no necessary connotation of bad health. "She has *fallen off* some, and looks much better." Cf. NID, *fall off*, f.

fanner: *n.* A basket, especially a broad flat basket for carrying fruit or vegetables. Formerly used when rice was threshed out with flails, to toss the rice into the air and allow the wind to fan out the chaff. Also called *fanner basket*. Norman Chamberlain suggests Lat. *vannus* as origin.

feather-legged: *adj.* Having feathers on the legs; hence, of cocks, a poor fighter. (Gamecocks have clean legs.) Hence, afraid to fight; cowed. The slogan of Judge Ira B. Jones, in his race for governor in 1912, was: "There are no feathers on my legs."

feed tree: *n.* A tree bearing fruit or berries, such as the persimmon or blackgum, which the opossum frequents to obtain food.

fiddle-footed: *adj.* Restive, given to wandering.

field lark: *n.* The meadow lark. NID, S. and C.

figater [fɪg'etə]: *n.* The Junebug, a persistent *fig eater*. Charleston.

figeater: *n.* The orchard oriole. S. and C. Cf. NID.

find: *v.i.* 1. To provide food, as for a party, a picnic. Cf. NID *find*, v.t., 8. 2. v.t. To give birth to, of persons or animals. "Liza *fin'* a chile last Wednesday." Cf. NID, *find* v.i. 9, v.t. 9.

fining: *pres. part.* Drizzling. "It's *fining* rain." So called because of the small or fine drops.

first Monday: *n.* A poor, worn-out, bony horse or mule, such as come up for public auction on the first Monday of each month.

fish eagle: *n.* The osprey. S. and C.

flat fish: *n.* Any fish of a short flat shape, as bream, warmouth, crappie, etc. Cf. NID.

Flemish account: *n.* A small amount. "There's a *Flemish account* of butter on the table tonight." Charleston. Origin undetermined.

flobert, flaubert [flobət]: *n.* Any small rifle, twenty-two caliber. Florence, S. C. Obsolescent? Once a popular make of rifle.

floor child, chile: *n.* A child old enough to be put on the floor.

flowsy ['flauzɪ]: *adj.* Untidy; slovenly. Cf. EDD, *floose*, a loose texture; *flowse*, flowing, flaunting; *flowsy*, sb., a slattern.

flutter mill: *n.* A toy made by children consisting of a *flutter wheel*, placed in a current of water so as to be turned by the current. A child's plaything in imitation of the water mill.

fly-in-the-milk: *n.* Offspring of one white and one colored parent. Alcolu.

fool sober: *adj.* Entirely and unreasonably sober. *Cold sober*, on the other hand, means *sober* in keeping with the seriousness of the occasion.

foot log: *n.* A log or beam laid across a stream from one bank to the other for use of pedestrians.

fork over: *v.t.* To give up, especially to pay money with a connotation of unwillingness. Bart.

forebay: *n.* The narrow, deep channel of water leading from the reservoir directly to the millwheel. Often pronounced *fo'bay.* Cf. NID.

frail: *v.t.* To flail, to beat with a flail; to beat. Usually of persons. NID, Wen.

frail: *n.* A long cudgel, a flail, usually for combat. NID, Wen.

fram: *v.t.* To drub, to pound, to beat. Wen.

franzy: *adj.* Delirious. Wen. Seneca and mountains. Variant of *frenzy.* EDD.

fraz: *n.* A very small portion or amount. "I'm worn to a *fraz.*" Cf. *frazzlings,* frayed out pieces or ends. May be connected with EDD, *frazy,* mean, niggardly, miserly, etc.

free issue: *n.* Offspring of white woman and Negro man. Sand hills of central S. C. and Pee Dee.

free trader: *n.* A wife to whom the husband has transferred his property to evade the payment of debt.

freight bird: *n.* The southern crested flycatcher. S. and C.

French candy: *n.* Any sort of candy in the shape and size of bonbons, such as chocolate drops, gum drops, etc., and including the small boxes of assorted bonbons and chocolates. French candy was contrasted with stick candy. Obsolescent.

French mockingbird: *n.* The loggerhead shrike. S. and C.

French mulberry: *n.* The Indian mulberry.

fresh: *n.* 1. Freshly butchered pork. Lexington and Saluda counties. 2. Any fresh meat, as game, etc. "Take dis meat sack an yo' gun, and git goin'. I ain't eat *fresh* in Gawd knows when."

frog lantern: *n.* A rectangular doughnut or cruller, pierced by slits, as if to permit the passage of light. Charleston.

frog spittle: *n.* Spirogyra. Also called *watersilk, frogum.* NID.

frogum: *n.* Children's name for Spirogyra. Supposed to be the excretion of frogs.

fudge: *v.i.* To take an illicit advantage, to take advantage secretly, on the sly, as in carrying out an agreement, a contract, etc. "The number is correct, but he fudged on us in the quality."

In playing marbles, to come closer to the target than the rules allow. Cf. NID, *fudge*, intrans., 5.

fully colored: *adj.* Neither sallow nor black, but ruddy brown. The color of the *Fulah* Negroes of French West Africa. Probably from *Fulah* colored, with the aid of folk etymology.

fus' day: *n.* First day. That is, broad daylight in the morning. Same as *day clean*.

fus' X: *n.* The cheapest grade of liquor sold by the S. C. dispensary in Tillman's days. *Fus' X* (first X) was marked in the bottle with one X and sold for fifteen cents a half pint. The four grades of corn liquor were marked with one, two, three or four X's. Obsolete.

gabble racket, gobble ratchet: *n.* The honking sound made by wild geese flying by night; employed with various supernatural meanings, as of witches' chatter on broomstick flights; anciently believed to be the crying of unbaptized children doomed to wander in space until Judgment Day. Cf. *Wild Hunt*, Hugo's *Les djinns*, Ger. *Die wilde Jagd*, the recent popular song, "Riders in the Sky," etc.

gallus: *n.* 1. A suspender for the trousers. Also pl. *galluses*. 2. The gallows. NID, Wen.

gambling strings: *n. pl.* The tendons on the hindlegs of slaughtered animals by which they are suspended by means of a *gambrel* for evisceration.

gamblin' stick: *n.* A gambrel. Wen.

garbroth: *n.* Only in the simile "mean as *garbroth*." The gar is not highly prized as an edible fish. Wen., under *gar*.

gallihootin: *adv.* Variant of *callihootin*.

gator tail: *n.* A single-handed crosscut saw. So called from its general shape.

Gawd's: *adj.* An illiterate use, mostly Gullah. "He ain't done a *Gawd's* thing." "I never ketch a *Gawd* swimp."

geech: *v.t.* To tease by touching about the ribs. Applies only to susceptible or *geechy* persons.

geechee, geechy ['gitʃi, 'gitʃɪ]: *n.* A low country term for a Negro. NID. "Wild Negroes fresh from Africa used to be put on *Ogeechee* river plantations in Georgia to mix with the hands there until they learned the minimum of white man's ways, that is, wearing clothes, a few English words, etc. Thus a *geechy* Negro means a Negro from an *Ogeechee* plantation." L. J. DuBose.

geechy: *adj.* Goosey, very nervous, unusually sensitive to geeching or tickling.

geechy limes: *n. pl.* "Preserved limes, said to be from the Ogeechee river of Georgia." Miss May Waring.

Georgia cabin: *n.* A two-room cabin with an open runway, called a *dog run* or a *dog trot* between the two rooms.

Georgia major: *n.* A pretentious fellow. A *Georgia major's* uniform is said to be a pair of spurs and a paper collar.

giffy ['gɪfɪ]: *adj.* Cloudy and damp, applied to the weather. Origin undetermined, possibly African.

'gin [gɪn]: *conj.* By the time that, as soon as, when. "Have supper ready *'gin* I get home." Elided form of *agin.* NID, *against,* conj. EDD, *again,* conj. and adv.

glacety ['glesɪtɪ]: *adj.* Scatterbrained. Obsolete. Anderson. Cf. *glace,* v., to glide, to skim by, graze, shave. EDD.

go seeking: *v.i.* To go in search of religion or conversion. "Ah *gwine seeking.*" Negro dialect.

go-devil: *n.* 1. An evil spirit, supposed to roam the woods at night, uttering weird cries. 2. A kind of fireworks. Coastal area.

gofer: *n* Waffle. Negro usage. St. John's Parish, Berkeley County. A Huguenot French survival. Fr. *gauffre,* waffle. Cf. NID, *gaufre.*

gone gosling: *n.* One who is beaten, checked, frustrated, "done for." Bart., *gone goose.*

goner: *n.* One who is hopelessly lost. Bart., Wen.

goober ['gʊbə, 'gubə]: *n.* Peanut. Kimbundu: *nguba,* peanut—Turner.

gooch: *v.t.* Same as *geech.* Seems to be a blend of *goose,* v.t., and *geech,* v.t.

goochy: *adj.* Goosey. Same as *geechy.* Probably a blend of *goosey* and *geechy.*

good: *n.* Good news, in the greeting: "What's all the *good?*" Conway.

goose drownder: *n.* A very heavy rain, a downpour. Cf. *lighterd knot floater, trash mover, gully washer.* Horry County.

gooseneck squash: *n.* The long, yellow, crooked-necked squash.

gorgeous: *adj.* Applied to articles of rich food, with which one's appetite is soon satisfied, and on which one is easily *gorged.* "Dat 'possum meat sho' is *gorgeous.*" Negro usage of southeast Georgia.

gorm: *n.* 1. An awkward deed; a stupid deed; a blunder. "To commit a *gorm*." 2. A mess; a state of confusion, disorder. Wen., EDD, *garm*, *gaum*.

gorm, gaum: *v.t.* 1. To soil with grease, molasses or otherwise, as the hands, the face, the clothing. "Your face is all *gaumed* up with jam." 2. To render untidy, as the dress, clothing. Wen., NID, EDD, *garm*, *gaum*.

gormandize: *v.i.* To eat carelessly and smear or *gorm* one's clothes in the process.

gormy, gaumy: *adj.* 1. Smeared, soiled. 2. Untidy; when a lady's stockings wrinkle around the ankle she is said to have *gormy* ankles.

gospel shoes: *n. pl.* Sunday shoes.

governor's gate: *n.* The gap left in a child's mouth where he has lost a front tooth. Also called *toll gate*.

grain: *n.* A drop of liquid. A fever patient begs for "just one *grain* of water to cool my parched mouth."

grainkind: *n.* Hominy or rice served as a cereal. "You ain't goin' to have no *grainkind* today?" James Island.

grampus: *n.* 1. An imaginary sea monster. Used humorously. "To catch a *grampus*." 2. The bottle-nosed dolphin. Cf. NID.

grand: *n.* A grandchild. Coastal Negro usage; also heard among upcountry whites.

granny: *n.* 1. A grandmother. 2. A midwife. 3. Any woman who assists at childbirth. NID.

granny: *v.t.* To act as midwife for; to work as a midwife. NID.

granny woman: *n.* Same as *granny*, n. 2 and 3.

grass: *n.* Asparagus. Shortened form of *sparrowgrass*, q.v.

gronnut, grounut ['grʌnət, 'graʊnət] **cake:** *n.* Groundnut cake; peanut meats mixed with cooked molasses. The molasses is cooked to a candied state. Similar to goober candy, peanut brittle, etc. Florence, Charleston. Used to be sold by colored vendors in Charleston to school children at recess, for one cent a cake.

grum and chuff: *adj.* Sulky in demeanor and surly in speech; morose and forbidding. Lower S. C. EDD, *grum*, *surly*, etc. See *chuff*. NID.

grumblesome: *adj.* Irritable, complaining, given to *grumbling*.

grunnut, grunnit ['grʌnət, 'grʌnɪt]: *n. Groundnut.* Charleston. See *grounut* cake.

guinea squash: *n.* The eggplant.

gully washer: *n.* A heavy downpour. Hill country. Wen.

gumbo: *n.* Boiled okra; okra soup. Origin uncertain. Turner, p. 194, suggests *chingumbo* [tʃiŋgɔmbɔ], okra. There are also other theories, as the *gummy* consistency of cooked okra.

gump: *n.* A silly, stupid or foolish person. NID, Wen.

gumption: *n.* Energy; common sense, understanding. NID, Wen., Bart., *PADS*, 13, p. 17.

gun-shy: *adj.* Cowardly. Probably a euphemistic expression from pioneer and Reconstruction days. Obsolete. From a *gun-shy* dog or horse.

gunjer ['gʌndʒə]: *n.* 1. Gingerbread. 2. A huge ginger cracker formerly sold in country stores. Gullah *ganja*, gingerbread. Turner suggests Hausa, *sakandjabir*, ginger, as the origin.

gunjer pone: *n.* A pone of gingerbread.

guyascutus: *n.* An imaginary monster. Cf. NID, *gyascutus.*

gwine: *pres. part.* Going "Whar you *gwine?*" When used as an auxiliary, *gwine* is often pronounced *gwi'*, with or without a nasalized *i.* "What you *gwi'* do 'bout it?"

gyarden, kyar, gyrl, gyard, kyards, etc. Dialect pronunciation of *garden, car, girl, guard, cards,* etc. A survival of an eighteenth-century pronunciation which is still heard in the coastal area, especially in Charleston, but only sporadically in the remainder of the state.

hack.: *n.* and *v.t.* To embarrass, to render ill at ease. "John's going courting. Don't say anything about it, or you'll *hack* him." As a noun; "to get, or keep a person under *hack.*" Wen.

hacked: *adj. past part.* Ill at ease, embarrassed. Wen.

hagfish: *n.* Stale fish peddled on the streets which, when eaten, cause ptomaine poisoning, are alleged by the peddlers to have been caught in the night by witches or *hags* flying over the river and plunging like seagulls on their prey, and thus to have been impregnated with a malevolent essence. Negro usage.

hag hollerin': *n.* The time of night when ghosts are supposed to walk and the graves to give up their dead.

hah-ah ['haʔˌa]: *n.* An exclamation of disapproval or warning, [ˌhaˈʔa] usually addressed only to children. The pronunciation of this word with the lips closed gives the familiar negation *hunh-unh* ['hʌ̃ʔˌʌ̃], and is probably the origin of this puzzling grunt. The opposite of the negation would then be produced by a similar development of the exclamation *aha* [ʔɑ'hɑ], which expresses pleasure, pleased surprise, discovery, etc., as well as simple astonishment, and the affirmative [ˌʔʌ̃'hʌ].

hairy head: *n.* The hooded merganser; the red-breasted merganser. S. and C.

half-a-shirt: *n.* The red-headed woodpecker. S. and C. Cf. *shirttail bird.*

half-bed: *n.* A single bed.

hambone: *n.* The bone of a pork ham after most of the meat has been sliced off. Hambones are then used for boiling with vegetables, dumplings, etc.

hamestrap: *n.* A leather strap with a buckle on one end, used to strap the hames together permanently at the top.

hamestring: *n.* A leathern thong about three feet long with a large knot on one end, used to tie the hames together at the lower ends. The hamestring is tied and untied each time the gear is put on and taken off an animal.

handstick: *n.* A stout pole, six to eight feet long, used in carrying heavy timber. The *handstick* is placed under the timber forward of the middle and one man lifts on either side. The tail end then is carried by one man who *tails* the burden. Two handsticks may also be used with four bearers. The dialect phrase "tote fair" (NID) means originally to hold the handstick the same distance from the log as your partner does. The bearer who is farther away from the burden has a lighter load, and is not "toting fair."

ha'nt [hænt]: *n.* A spirit, supernatural being, whose main object is to frighten people. A ghost is supposed to be the spirit of some dead person, but the *ha'nt* has ordinarily no such association. However, a ghost may *ha'nt* a mortal, that is, appear to him and frighten him to avenge some wrong.

Dogs may be misled at night by a *ha'nt.* Small trees bent down to the ground in the forest, especially small pines, the effect of a freezing rain, are supposed to be the work of *ha'nts,* for although a *ha'nt* is impalpable and without weight, it can supposedly bend down the largest trees at will. Wen.

"I have hunted 'possums with a Gullah Negro and seen the dog trail around and around in circles. Cuffy would say, 'Dat ain't nuttin but a *ha'nt* leadin' dat dog 'roun.' Then he would call the dog in, strike a match and make the sign of the Cross three times on the dog's forehead. The *ha'nt*, being frightened by the sulphur in the match would disappear for the night. *'Ha'nt 'feard* sulphur too much ['tʌmɪtʃ].'" C. M. McKinnon.

ha'nt: *v.t.* To inhabit or frequent a house, locality, etc., such as the churchyard. Said of ghosts or *ha'nts*. Wen.

ha'nted: *past part. adj.* Haunted, frequented by ghosts or *ha'nts*.

hard: *n.* Dry land; a careenage. *"On the hard,"* on dry land or sound gravel beach. "To put a boat *on the hard*," to haul out of the water for painting, calking, repair, or winter storage.

harricane: *n.* A tree uprooted by the wind. Curruption of *hurricane*. NID, Wen.

harry dick: *n.* 1. Baby beef. Harry dick has the flavor neither of veal nor of full grown beef, and is less desirable than either. The Florida cattleman's term for a maverick is *hairydick*, whence probably our phrase. 2. A castrated beef of about yearling age. 3. The devil. "The old *Harry Dick*." 4. An adolescent boy. Cf. Wen.

heabe: *v.t.* To heave; *"heabe* a sifer," heave a sigh. Coastal Negro usage.

head: *n.* In numbering, applied to persons as well as animals. "Six *head* of chillun."

hellcat: *n.* A woman of unbridled temper or tongue; a fighting woman. Not otherwise derogatory.

hell-hack: *v.t.* To worry, to annoy. Cf. *hell-hackle*.

hell-hackle: *v.t.* To cow; to depress, to dishearten. Cf. NID, *hackle*, vt. and v.i.

hell-hackled: *past part. adj.* Depressed, dispirited, discouraged, cowed.

hershel: *v.t.* To call coaxingly, as a dog. Origin undetermined.

het: *adj. past part.* Heated; angry; excited. Usually with *up*. A popular form on the analogy of *meet: met, bleed: bled*, etc.

hickory: *n.* Any kind of switch, hickory or otherwise, used as a rod of correction.

hickory nut: *n.* The nut of a certain variety of hickory trees. The *hickory nut* has an oblong, slightly flattened shape, with a four-ridged exterior, a thick shell and small kernel. The *pig nut* is of the same size, is more flattened and has a smooth surface. The kernel is a slight bit larger than that of the *hickory nut*. The *scaly bark* (NID, *shagbark*) is a smaller nut with the general shape of the hickory nut, but with a much thinner shell and larger kernel. See NID, Bart.: *shell bark, shagbark.*

hickory shirt: *n.* A work shirt made of heavy cotton material. Bart.

highcockalorum: *n.* A disrespectful name referring to a person of real or assumed importance. NID.

hill: *n.* Land above water, not covered by high tides, or by freshets in a river. Coastal area.

hime hister ['haɪm 'haɪstə]: *n.* Song leader who "hists" the hymns, "raises the tunes." Also *song hister, tune hister.*

hind sights: *n. pl.* In the expression "to knock the *hind sights* out of ..." to deal a destructive blow to a person or thing, to knock to pieces. Probably refers originally to the *hind sights* of a gun.

hippins: *n. pl.* Diapers (*hip* garments). NID, *hipping.*

hippo syrup: *n.* Syrup of ipecacuanha. A medical term familiar fifty years ago, but surviving only among the old or sequestered. The cockney English mariners who first reported the native remedy pronounced it *hippecac*, whence *hippo syrup.* Charleston and environs.

hist, hise [haɪst, haɪs]: *v.t.* A form of *hoist.* Cf. *pint* for *point, jint* for *joint.* To raise, to hoist. "Kin you *hist* that tune?" Wen., NID.

hit: *pron. It.* This Anglo-Saxon form still persists among the unlettered.

hit the grit: *v.i.* 1. To run, especially to run away. 2. To fall from a blow; also, *hit the dirt.*

hodgepodge: *n.* Mush, made of corn meal. Orangeburg. Cf. NID.

hoecake: *n.* A corn meal cake, originally under primitive conditions, baked on a hoe; a corn meal cake baked on a griddle. NID, Bart.

hog head cheese: *n.* Same as *souse.* The word *headcheese* is seldom heard alone.

hog killin': *n.* Freshly butchered pork meat, including souse, sausage, brains, cracklings, etc. Sumter. Cf. *fresh.*

hog killin': *adj.* Hog killing time is a season of severe and lasting cold weather, required for the preserving of the meat; also a time of plenty and rejoicing.

hollow-horn: *n.* "This and *hollow-tail* are names given in certain sections to a condition in cattle which causes them to be off feed or just plain sick. There are no such diseases, and the condition is usually the symptom of some sickness. Crude treatments, such as boring a hole in the horns, or splitting the base of the tail and rubbing the wound with salt, are resorted to, but the treatment is worthless and is rapidly becoming extinct." L. S. Wolfe, *Farm Glossary*, 1948. (Correspondents say there are still many who are convinced of the reality of these two diseases.)

hollow-tail: *n.* See *hollow-horn.*

holp [hop]: *v. pret.* and *past part.* of *help.*

holy laugh: *n.* A mirthless laugh uttered by anyone during a religious meeting.

hominy: *n.* Coarseground maize prepared for table use; grits; *hominy* grits. The *hominy* of trade, or hulled corn, is here called *big hominy* or *lye hominy.* Cornmeal so prepared for the table is called *mush.*

honeyfunk: *v.t.* and *v.i.* To deceive by flattery; to curry favor, especially of a student with a professor or with the authorities. Expresses great contempt. Columbia, especially on the campus of the University of S. C. Appears in the Clemson annual, *Taps,* of 1914, and is reported from Clemson as late as 1926. *Honeyfunk* is a variant of *honeyfogle, honeyfugle,* from *honey,* to flatter and EDD *fugle,* to cheat, deceive, trick.

hooey [huɪ]: *interj.* Used to frighten cattle out of one's way. Cf. NID, Wen.

hook-hand: *adv.* Arm in arm. "To walk *hook-hand* . . ."

hoop, whoop [huːp, hwuːp]: *excl.* A call to hogs and pigs. "Whoop, pig, pig!" General. In some places, however, the exclamation *sooey* is used to call hogs.

hoot owl: *n.* The great horned owl; the Florida barred owl. S. and C.

[3] **hoppin' John:** *n.* Rice and cowpeas cooked together, usually with a piece of bacon or a hambone or some other sort of pork. *Limpin' Kate* is formed on the analogy of *hoppin' John.* Cf. Bart.:

[3] Hoppin' John is probably on most tables in S. C. on New Year's Day. This with collard greens is supposed to bring the family plenty of greenbacks and loose change throughout the year. It is believed that one is tempting fate if one fails to have hoppin' John on the table New Year's Day.

"A stew of bacon and peas with red pepper" (1857). Probably from *pois à pigeon* of Jamaica, although other derivations have been proposed. Mr. Samuel G. Stoney reports this from the late Langdon Cheves.

horning: *pres. part* and *gerund.* Blowing snuff through a paper cone into the nostril of a woman in labor to hasten delivery of the child. The verb, *to horn,* is not reported so far. Lancaster County. Cf. *quilling,* used in the Ozarks.

horny: *adj.* Sexually excited; easily excited in a sexual sense. Only of males. Wen.

horse cake: *n.* A sweet cake, cut in the shape of a horse and baked.

horse gunjer: *n.* A gingercake in the shape of a horse. Obsolescent. Charleston.

hot: *v.t.* To heat. NID, Wen.

hotten: *v.t.* To heat. "*Hotten* up the coffee."

house moss: *n.* Collection of dusty, downy fibers found under furniture where one does not often sweep. Same as "kitties," (Wentworth lists "Kittens"). *Slut's wool* and *snorf,* with the same meaning, carry a strong connotation of reproach.

how come: *adv.* For what reason, why. "*How come* he didn't want to go?" "He didn't say *how come.*" Wen. Gullah form, *hukkuh.*

hug-me-tight: *n.* 1. A buggy, with a narrow seat, so as to give barely room for two. Obsolescent. 2. The scapula of a chicken or turkey and the portion of meat thereon. Sometimes applied to the wishbone. Cf. NID, Wen.

hulgul ['hʌl'gʌl]: *n.* A children's game. One child holds out a closed hand with peas, beans, marbles, etc., in it and says "hulgul." The other player says "handful." Then the first player asks: "How many?" If the other player guesses the exact number of units, he gets them all. If not, he pays out the difference between his guess and the right number. Then the other player begins.

hundred: *n.* District, neighborhood. "How are things in your *hundred?*" "A small political division derived from the English county division," NID, *hundred,* n. 7. Williamsburg County.

hunker: *v.i.* To squat, to sit in a squatting position; also noun: "sitting on his *hunkers,*" squatting down (Scotticism). EDD, NID.

hunnah, hoonah: *pron.* You, singular or plural. Same as *yunnah.* Gonz.: *wunnah, hoonuh, oonuh.*

hurrah's nest: *n.* Anything presenting an untidy, disorderly, and neglected appearance. "Her hair looked like a *hurrah's nest.*" NID, Wen.

hush puppies: *n. pl.* Corn meal cakes fried in deep grease. One recipe is to make a batter of corn meal and flour in proportion of four to one, mixed with cream, condensed milk or milk, flavoring with finely cut onions and red pepper. Add baking powder at the last and drop with a large spoon into the deep fat. There are many recipes. Same as *red horse bread* except that the latter is fried in the same fat in which fish have been fried. From the *hush* that prevails when dogs, barking with hunger, receive their daily meal.

hutzel: *n.* Clingstone peach dried on the kernel by cutting through the pulp and exposing to the sun. Peaches are thus kept for cooking purposes in the winter. Dutch Fork. Ger. *hutzel, etwas eingedorrtes, geschrumpftes* (something dried, shriveled).

hyonder: *adj.* and *adv.* There, yonder, e.g. over *hyonder.* Cf. *whelp (whelt)* for *welt, overhalls* for *overalls,* etc. Cf. Wen. p. 201, excrescent *h.*

Indian bread: *n.* The truffle. Cf. NID and Bart. under *Tuckahoe.*

Indian peach: *n.* A cling-stone peach with reddish color and dusky-red streaks, the flesh of which is also streaked with red.

Indian pullet: *n.* The king rail. S. and C.

infare: *n.* The reception given to a wedding party at the home of the groom. It followed the wedding party at the house of the bride. Obsolescent. NID.

ingans, inguns: *n. pl.* Onions. Seldom heard in singular form. NID.

ishters ['aɪʃtəz]: *n. pl.* Oysters. Beaufort, and probably along the coast.

invite ['ɪnvaɪt]: *n.* An invitation. NID.

innards: *n. pl.* Intestines, viscera, inwards. NID, Wen.

jack Mormon: *n.* A person born a Mormon but who does not live up to rules of the church, especially as regards drinking, smoking, etc. Cf. *"jackleg* carpenter," *"jack* of all trades," etc.

jarhead: *n.* A mule. Wen.

jaybird gossip: *n.* The petty scandals of the backyard, malicious and amusing like the raucous chatter of the jays.

jeans: *n. pl.* A heavy, close woven, dark gray woolen material used for making men's and boys' winter clothing. Cf. NID, *jean, jeans.* Farmers formerly had a flock of sheep whose wool was sheared and sent to a factory, for which the farmer received a bolt of jeans. The practice may still prevail in some sections. The twilled cotton is also called *jeans*, not *jean*.

jerked up: *past part. adj.* Grown up without breeding, rearing, training. *Jerk* is often pronounced *jeck,* and on the coast, *juck* [dʒʌk].

jessamy wine: *n.* The jessamine vine. In Negro speech, *v* is often sounded like *w,* especially in lower S. C., *Summerwille* for *Summerville,* etc.

jew down: *v.t.* To beat down the seller's price in buying. Bart., to *jew,* to cheat.

jewlark: *n.* A sweetheart. Connected with *lark,* to sport, frolic.

jice, jist [dʒaɪs, dʒaɪst]: *n.* A *joist.* Cf. *hist,* etc. Wen.

jimcrow cards: *n. pl.* Small wool cards used by Negroes to comb out their hair. "A familiar article in trade forty years ago, but little sold today." John Bennett.

jim-swinger: *n.* A long-tailed coat. Wen.

jimmie-jawed: *adj.* a variant of *jimber-jawed.*

jimble-jawed: *adj.* Having a long face with a sad expression. "Whut makes you look so *jimble-jawed?*"

Job's tears: *n. pl.* A string of *Job's tears* used as a rosary. Cf. NID.

joggling board: *n.* A heavy, supple board about ten inches wide, ten to twenty feet long, supported at each end at a height of eighteen to twenty-four inches, on which children *joggle* up and down in play. Formerly often seen on the front porch, now less common. Cf. Bart., *jiggling-board, jolly-board.*

Johnny cockhorse, Johnny cockaw, Johnny crookhorse: *n.* The praying mantis.

joog [dʒʊg]: *v.t.* To prod, to punch. "If I go to sleep in church, you *joog* me in the side." Wen.

joree: *n.* The green-tailed towhee. S. and C.

jove: *v.i.* To joke, to indulge in pleasantry or raillery. "Now le's we *jove* an' mek funny!" Adj., jovial, cheerful, gay. "We all love Mauss' Willie . . . he ben so *jove* all de time." Negro usage.

juba: *n.* A Negro dance. "Min' yo' manners, chile, or I'll mek you dance *juba!*" Cf. Bart., NID, Wen. See *pat juba.*

juberous, jubus ['dʒubərəs, 'dʒubəs]: *adj.* Doubtful, *dubious.* "A *juberous* plan." Undecided, hesitant, uncertain. "He's still *juberous* about going." Corruption of *dubious.* Wen.

Judas bird: *n.* The dickcissel, the black-throated bunting. S and C. Origin undetermined.

Judas goat: *n.* "Trained goat, used by slaughter houses to lead sheep to the killing pen." L. S. Wolfe, *Farm Glossary*, 1948.

jugfull: *n.* A great deal. "Not by a *jugfull*," not by a "long sight." Bart.

juice: *v.t.* To extract the juice from. "*Juice* me these lemons."

juke box: *n.* An automatic record-playing music box operated by a slot machine. A "piccolo" or "nickelodeon." For the word *juke*, as in *juke box*, *juke joint*, Turner, p. 195, suggests: Wolof, *jug*, to lead a disorderly life; Bambara, *jugu*, wicked, violent, a naughty person.

Kate: *n.* The southern pileated woodpecker. S. and C. Cf. NID.

ketch: *n.* and *v.t.* To catch. Also noun: "A good *ketch* of fish." Rather general, not limited to illiterates. "Typical fronting of slack front vowels in S. C." R. W. Achurch.

kettle tea: *n.* 1. Cambric tea, tea made of hot water, milk and sugar. 2. Plain hot water, with or without sugar, which some people drink, usually before breakfast, for their health. Wen.

kick: *v.t.* To jilt. Bart., Wen.

kink: *v.i.* 1. To lose one's breath in a tantrum of crying. Said of children; to lose one's breath in a fit of laughter. 2. *v. refl.* To lose one's breath by drinking in a strained position, as when drinking from a spring or stream. "Don't drink too long, or you'll *kink* yourself." EDD, NID.

kitties: *n. pl.* Same as *house moss., q.v.* Wen., *kitten.* Sumter County.

knee child: *n.* A child old and strong enough to play about its mother's knees.

knock out: *n.* A brilliant success, as a public presentation, play, etc. Less often, of persons, a handsome appearance.

knock up: *v.t.* To make pregnant. Of unmarried women. See under *trouble*.

knuckle down: *v.i.* To bend all one's energies to the task. "I've got to *knuckle down* and finish." Cf. NID. Perhaps borrowed from the game of marbles.

kraut: *n.* Cabbage. Dutch Fork. German, *kraut*, cabbage.

krex: *v.i.* To fret. "The baby is *krexin'*." Origin undetermined. Probably a German dialect word.

kronky: *n.* The sandhill crane. S. and C. Origin undetermined.

kwile: *v.t.* and *v.i. Coil.* "The snake was *kwiled.*"

kyarn crow [kjɑnkro]: *n. Carrion crow.* Analogous to *kyar,* for *car,* etc.

lace jacket: *n.* A corset.

lady fingers: *n. pl.* Same as *marvelle, q.v.* Cf. NID.

Lafayette cakes: *n. pl.* Small rectangular sweetcakes first peddled through the streets of Charleston to signalize the visit of Gen. Lafayette in 1825. Last served by the Charleston Museum at an event which marked the general's visit. Cakes and name obsolescent.

lalla: *adj.* Careless, indifferent. "He acted in a *lalla* manner." Coastal.

lalla shop ['lælə]: *n.* A small, perhaps disreputable shop catering to a low grade patronage, dealing in cheap miscellany, second-hand wares and clothing. See *lalla,* adj.

lallygag ['læligæg]: *n.* Chatter, idle talk. Cf. Wen. Combination of *lalling* and *gaggle,* n.

lallygag, lollygag: *v.i.* To chatter, talk idly. Cf. Wen.

land doctor: *n.* An engineer or surveyor. He is supposed to cut up the land, as a doctor cuts up people. Negro usage. Charleston.

lantern-jawed: *adj.* Having long thin jaws and hollow cheeks. Cf. NID. Origin undetermined.

lap child, chile: *n.* An infant.

larnin': *n.* Learning. An illiterate use still occasionally heard, especially in the combination "book *larnin.*" Wen.

Lawd-Gawd: *n. Lord God.* The pileated woodpecker. "So called in Negro dialect because of his impressive look." This derivation is suggested by Mr. C. M. McKinnon. Another name for this bird is *logcock,* of which our entry may be a corruption. However, the fact that this bird is also known among the Negroes of the *Pee-Dee* as *Doctor Jesus,* lends support to Mr. McKinnon's theory.

lay: *v.i.* To lie. "he *laid* down on the ground and went to sleep." The strong intransitives *rise, sit, lie,* are rapidly being displaced by their weak causative forms, *raise, set, lay.*

lay-by time: *n.* Fourth of July to Labor Day, when cotton crops are too mature to be cultivated and are not ready for picking. In Chesterfield County called *bustin'-out-the-middle time.*

lay-over: *n.* A trap. Used only in the expression: "A *layover* to catch meddlers," and here only in answer to some idle or impertinent question, such as: "What is that?" "What are you making?" This form, however, has been corrupted in popular speech into: *laros, naro, lairs, larovus*. Wentworth cites many other variants. The *lay-over* is defined as a pit covered with branches to catch bears. NID, Wen.

laying-down time: *n.* Bedtime.

lazy boy: *n.* A hand-operated blade for cutting weeds and grass. It has a very long handle and doesn't require stooping.

lazy Susan: *adj.* and *n.* A *lazy Susan* table is a round dinner table having a revolving element on which viands may be turned from one diner to another; the revolving element of such a table. NID.

leatherback: *n.* The ruddy duck. NID, S. and C.

leather breeches: *n.* The ruddy duck. S. and C.

leather breeches beans: *n. pl.* String beans dried for winter consumption. So called because of the leathery appearance and texture. Wen.

left: *n.* In the phrase, *over the left*, meaning dubious, false, deceitful, said of a promise not meant to be kept, a threat that is futile on its face, a boast incapable of fulfillment. A contemptuous commentary upon anything evidently untrue. Bart., *over the left*.

let on: *v.i.* To betray one's knowledge of a question, a situation, a fact or circumstance under discussion. "While we were talking about the ruckus, he stood there and never *let on* that he was in it." Used only in a negative sentence or in a question expecting a negative answer. Wen., Bart.

level: *n.* In the phrase *on the level*, sincere, honest, straightforward; just.

lief: *n.* Leave, permission. "You can't bend my arm." "You gimme *lief?*" Do you give me *leave* to try it? NID, Wen.

lighterd: *n. Lightwood*. Wen.

lighterd knot: *n.* A knot or rich pine used as lightwood.

lights: *n.* Lungs of a slaughtered animal. In the expression "to knock one's *lights* out" the word may refer to the human lungs. Cf. NID.

lightwood: *n.* Wood suitable for kindling a fire, especially heart pine rich in rosin. Formerly used to make a *light*. NID.

limb: *n.* The leg. Obsolescent. NID, Bart.

limbless: *adj.* Unable to use one's legs.

line dam: *n.* A "dam" formed by the spoil from a boundary ditch. Coastal area.

line ditch: *n.* A ditch marking a property line.

liquor head: *n.* A drunkard.

little blue darter: *n.* The sharp-shinned hawk. S. and C.

little indigo: *n.* The indigo bunting. S. and C.

little sapsucker: *n.* The southern downy woodpecker. S. and C.

limpin' Kate, limpin' Kit: *n.* Cowpeas and hominy cooked together. See *hoppin' John.*

lippin: *v.i.* To trust, to have faith. "You don't have to understand, just *lippin.*" EDD.

locus: *adj.* Local. Only in the phrase *"locus* preacher." General Negro usage. Probably Southwide.

logy [logɪ]: *adj.* Dull, inert, slow. Used to describe a person's feelings. "After a heavy meal I feel *logy.*" NID, Bart., Wen., *logey.*

long-o'-de-paat chillun [ˌlɔŋ-ə-də-ˈpæːt]: *n. pl.* Illegitimate children. Children begotten *along the path.* Negro usage.

long sweetening: *n.* Molasses used as sweetening for drinks, as coffee, tea, etc., or in cooking. Bart., NID, Wen.

lose the cud: *phr.* When a cow stops ruminating she is said to have *lost her cud.* "Not a disease but merely a symptom of some derangement." L. S. Wolfe, *Farm Glossary.*

lowgrounds: *n. pl.* Bottoms, bottom land.

low-rate: *v.t.* To deprecate; to set a low estimate on. Usually of persons. Wen.

lye hominy: *n.* Hulled corn. Also called *big hominy.* In the trade called *hominy.*

magnolia bird: *n.* The red-eyed vireo. S. and C.

man: *n.* Physical strength; superior powers, physical or otherwise. "How did you get the piano in here?" "I did it *on my man.*" "He stopped that mob by himself *on his man.*" Compare the phrase: *man enough to. . . .*

manifac [ˈmænɪfæk]: *adj. Manufactured,* as contrasted with homemade. *"Manifac* smoking tobacco," etc.

manussable [ˈmænəsəbḷ]: *adj.* Courteous, polite, having good manners. (*Manners-able*). Charleston. Wen. *Mannersable.*

marsh tacky: *n.* A small pony raised in the low country. A term of derision. See *tacky.*

marvelle [mɑˈvɛl]: *n.* Rectangular cake of sweet dough slit several times lengthwise and fried. The slit sections are usually twisted, probably to allow the frying fat to penetrate more easily.

Also called *lady fingers*. Cf. F. & W. '25: *lady's finger*, n. 1. A small cake, so called from its shape. Cf. NID.

mash: *v.i.* To apply pressure. With prep. *on.* "His ankle is so much better he can *mash on* it a little." 2. *v.t.* To strike against an obstacle. "He *mashed* his foot on a rock." Negro usage.

'matos, 'matises ['metəs, 'metɪsɪz]: *n. pl.* Tomatoes.

mauma ['mɔːmə]: *n.* 1. Name by which elderly Negro women were called by the children of the family with which they were connected. When the name followed the title, the final *a* was elided: "*Maum'* Dinah." In the upcountry this title of respect was *aunty* and *aunt.* 2. An overgrown, two-year-old potato.

maussa ['mɔːsə]: 1. *v.t.* To command, to order about, as the master was supposed to do in the days of *Uncle Tom's Cabin.* 2. *n.* Master, in slavery days.

Mayo: *n.* A great water or river, as the River of Death. Negro songs, probably spirituals, contained the phrase to "cross the mighty *Mayo*," and find rest in the bosom of God. Obsolete or obsolescent. Beaufort County. Origin uncertain.

maze: *n.* Amazement. "Mek *maze*," to show delighted surprise. Coastal Negro usage. Cf. NID, EDD, *amaze, amazement,* wonder.

meet: *v.t.* To find. "I *meet* um gone," "I found them gone, they were gone when I arrived." "I *meet* um here when I come," "I found them here when I came." Negro usage, chiefly coastal area.

'member: *v.t.* To remind. "*'Member* me to call Jenny." Wen. under *remember.*

'member service: *n.* A religious service in *remembrance* of the dead, usually held on the first anniversary of death. Negro usage.

'member yaws: *n. pl.* A recurrent attack of frambesia.

mince: *v.t.* To eat without appetite, in a gingerly way; to eat fastidiously. "He's only *mincing* his food." Cf. NID, *mince,* v.t. 1, and Wen., *mincy.*

mind: *n.* Attention. "He don't pay me no *mind.*"

mirate: *v.i.* To make a miration over; to express surprise, admiration over a person or thing. Wen., NID.

miration: *n.* 1. Favorable attention; fuss; to-do. In the phrase "to make a *miration* over something," in a favorable sense. 2. Expression of surprise, astonishment, whether favorable or not. Wen.

mislist: *v.t.* To mistrust, suspect. Obsolete.

missed-meal colic: *n.* Hunger.

mockingbird tales: *n. pl.* Loose tattle of one who receives a bit of scandal in confidence and proceeds to broadcast it as the *mockingbird* does its borrowed songs.

molasses: *n. pl.* "*These molasses,*" "*them molasses,*" etc. Upper S. C.

molasses biscuit: *n.* A biscuit of an earlier period, about the size of an ordinary bakery roll, with a hole thrust into it from the side with the forefinger. The hole is then filled with molasses. A favorite of country children after school and in general between meals. Probably obsolete. Cf. *was' nes'*.

moldoshers ['mɑl͵dɑʃəz]: *n. pl.* Dumplings made of young spring onions and cooked with a hambone. Newberry County.

molly: *n.* The warmouth.

monkey: *n.* In the phrase "the *monkey,* or *monkeys,* got him," meaning he has been overcome by the heat. Also "the *bear* got him," in the same sense.

monkeys: *n.* Delirium tremens. "To have the *monkeys.*"

moody-colored: *adj.* Of a dull or sad color.

moonbill: *n.* The ring-necked duck. NID, S. and C.

moonshine: *n.* The common night heron. So called on account of its nocturnal habits.

more: *adj.* and *adv., comparative.* Often used in double comparatives; "*more sooner,*" "*more better,*" "*more older,*" etc.

morgan: *n.* The warmouth, a species of fresh water fish.

moses boat: *n.* A large flat used in lightering vessels anchored in the roadstead, and in other days for freighting rice barrels or cotton bales from plantation to port. NID, *moses.*

mosshead: *n.* The hooded merganser. NID, S. and C.

mother patch: *n.* Since the smoothest and best keeping sweet potatoes are grown from cuttings, a *mother patch* of plants is set out as early as possible and fertilized for rapid vine growth. From these vines of the *mother patch* cuttings are then secured for general planting.

mother potatoes: *n. pl.* The potatoes from which potato slips are grown for planting.

mousey ['maʊsɪ]: *adj.* Meddlesome, with a connotation of mouse-like slyness; of a girl: shy, bashful.

mouth, mouf [maʊθ, maʊf]: *n.* Bad luck; only in the phrase *to put mouf on,* to conjure, and cause to have bad luck. Implied is the pronunciation of some magic formula over a person, or against him. Cf. *bad moul', Black Border,* p. 288.

mouth-wash: *n.* A drink of liquor. Used during prohibition as an evasion. Obsolete (?).

muck: *n.* 1. A snarl, a tangle. "That backlash has my line in a *muck.*" 2. A state of confusion or uncertainty. "He is in a *muck* over what to do about the boll weevil." Cf. Wen., *muck,* v.

mudge: *v.i.* To move along slowly; to work in a leisurely way. Usually with the adv. *along.* Cf. NID. Aiken County, obsolescent.

muffle-jawed: *adj.* Having heavy, fleshy jaws. From NID, *muffle,* n. 5.

mug: *n.* A chamber.

muley ['mɪulɪ, 'mulɪ]: *adj.* Hornless, of cattle, like a mule. In upper S. C. pronounced *mooley.* Wen.

mumble peg: *n.* The game of *mumble-the-peg, mumblety-peg.* Cf. Bart., NID.

mummock, mommock, mommick; *v.t.* 1. To make a mess of, to spoil, to confuse. Used with the preposition *up.* "You certainly have got this job *mommocked up* to a fare-you-well!" 2. To browbeat, to harass. Wen.

muscovados: *n. pl.* A dark molasses obtained in the process of sugar refining, formerly a common article of the grocery trade. The plural form is probably due to the fact that in the dialect of upper S. C. *molasses* is plural. Cf. NID.

musk cat: *n.* The polecat, the skunk. Cf. NID.

muss: *v.t.* To disarrange, as the hair or clothing. Usually with *up.* NID, Bart., Wen.

mutton cane: *n.* Early growth of cane, excellent for forage. NID. Cf. *mutton corn.*

mutton corn: *n.* "Early Indian corn, still in the milk used for the table; roasting ears. Old Santee French *matin,* i.e. early." John Bennett.

nappy: *adj.* Of growing cotton, having bolls immaturely open, showing the locks of cotton only partly. NID, *nappy,* adj.

nary, nairy ['nærɪ]: *adj. Ne'er a.* No, not a. "Don't you pay him *nary* red cent." Wen.

nephew: *n.* A nephew or a niece. Coastal Negro usage.

newground: *n.* A piece of wooded land cleared for cultivation. A newground produces excellent crops the first year or two.

niece: *n.* A niece or a nephew. Coastal Negro usage.

niggerhead: *n.* 1. A metal casting, resembling a head and neck, bolted to a dock and used to make vessels fast with ropes or hawsers. 2. Cobblestones used in paving a road for heavy traffic. Cf. NID, *niggerhead*, 3 and 7.

nigger toe: *n.* The Brazil nut. NID.

nigger trader: *n.* A white man who bought stolen goods from slaves. Contemptuous. Obsolete.

niggle: *v.t.* and *v.i.* To fail; to cause to fail. Cf. NID, *niggle*, v.i.

nigh: *adj.* Near, close.

nigh: *adv.* Near. The older expression *nigh unto* has become now *nigh on to*: "He is *nigh on to* fifty." "It's *nigh on to* four miles from here." "Purty *nigh*, pu'ty *nigh*," ['pʊrtɪ, 'pʊtɪ], very nearly.

night glass: *n.* Same as *mug.*

night jar: *n.* Same as *mug.*

night look: *n.* The stupid expression on the face of a dull or drowsy person. Charleston.

ninny: *n.* 1. Milk from the breast. Child's language. 2. Hence, a cry-baby. Wen., NID.

no-count: *adj.* Worthless; of person: lazy, shiftless, worthless. NID. Shortened down from the phrase *of no account.*

noggin: *n.* The head, used familiarly and only of human beings.

nohow: *adv.* In no way. Usually at the end of a negative sentence, making a double negative. "I couldn't fix it *nohow*." NID, Wen., Bart.

no-mannus: *adj.* Ill mannered. "You want to grow up to be a *no-mannus* somebody?"

noon: *n.* The hour from noon to one o'clock taken by workers for lunch and as a rest period. "Don't you take no *noon?*" Edisto region.

noon: *v.i.* To take a nap at the *noon* hour. Edisto region.

no-rate: *v.t.* To rate as a nonentity.

nub, knub: *n.* The stump of a truncated limb, as a finger, arm, or leg. Cf. NID.

old hog: *n.* A half-pint bottle of corn whiskey with the palmetto blown in the glass, said to have been formerly sold by the S. C. dispensary at ten cents a bottle. Obsolete. A similar half-pint flask, especially of bootleg liquor, is called a *bat wing.*

old scratch: *n.* The devil. This term is not used in a jocular tone as is *Old Nick*, but is rather an evasion of the word *devil*, and is used seriously. Cf. NID.

old one-one: *n.* The eastern red-winged blackbird. So called from the habit of the two sexes to gather into separate flocks in the fall and winter seasons.

'oman: *n.* A woman. Mostly Negro usage, except for the phrase "*ol' 'oman,*" which is fairly general. Wen.

one: *adj.* Alone, only. "Nobody here but me *one.*" Negro usage of Charleston.

one-gallus: *adj.* Having only *one gallus,* hence not fastidious in dress; applied only to country people, and connoting closely the expression "grass roots." Not ordinarily used in derision. Often with political implications: "the *one-gallus* crowd," "the *one gallus* vote."

one-man match: *n.* Safety match. It strikes only on its own box. Cf. *one-man* dog, *one-man* woman, etc. Negro, coastal area.

one-one: *adj.* Normal; as usual. "How you stan' today?" "Kinda *one-one.*" Negro usage.

onliest: *adj.* Only.

ornery, onnery ['ɔnərɪ, 'ɑnərɪ]: *adj.* Ordinary, common, in the derogatory sense. Of persons: trifling, shiftless, indolent. Of behavior: disreputable, degrading. Of things: worthless, more troublesome than useful, "more trouble than they are worth."

ortolan: *n.* The sora. S. and C.

out: *v.t.* To extinguish, as a lamp, a fire. NID, Bart., Wen.

outen: *v.t.* To extinguish, as a fire. To erase, as writing on a slate. Wen.

outside plumbing: *n.* A euphemism for no plumbing, a privy.

overhalls: *n. Overalls.* Cf. *hyonder.*

owdacious [aʊ'deʃəs], **outdacious:** *adj.* Bold, audacious; unrestrained; outrageous. Wen., Bart. This seems to be a blend of *audacious* and *outrageous.* EDD, under *audacious.*

owdaciously: *adv.* In an *owdacious* manner.

own: *adj.* Used in a redundant possessive, not emphatic: "Mary's *own* is better than yours."

ownt: *adj.* Same as *own,* q.v. "Who *ownt* dis is?" Whose is this? Cf. Wen.: *own,* adj. Cf. Wen., under excrescent *t.*

paat [pæːt]: *n.* A *path.* See under *tief.*

pack: *v.t.* To carry. "The children *pack* their books to school." Mountains. NID, Wen.

pan squash: *n.* The cymling. So named from its shape.

parable: *n.* A wise statement. Mostly in the phrase: "You have spoken, or you spoke a parable."

paratoed: *adj. Parrot-toed,* a milder degree of pigeon-toed. NID, *parrot-toed.*

pass and repass: *v.i.* "We *pass and repass*," i.e., we are on fairly friendly terms.

pat juba: *v.t.* "The *juba* dance is said to have been a singular dance characteristic of *Adjuba* Negroes, and peculiar to that African tribe. It consisted of a difficult pattern of chassees, leaps and bucking movements, conforming to a difficult and unvariable pattern of hand clapping by two performers, who sat closely facing each other and smacked thighs, knees, and mutual hands after a rapid and very intricate design, hard to follow, very fast and most intriguing." John Bennett.

peart [pjɛət]: *adj.* Bright, cheerful, lively, able to get about. Said especially of people not expected to be able to move about much, as of the aged, the convalescent, etc. NID, Wen., Bart., under *peert*, and *PADS*, 11, p. 45.

peahams: *n. pl.* Pea-hulls. Cf. NID: *haulm*. . .straw or litter, also *ham*, a variant.

peckerwood: *n.* The woodpecker. Upper S. C. NID, Wen. "Peckerwood, whut make yo' head so red?" "Peckin' in the hot sun, nuthin' on my head." C. M. McKinnon.

peef: *v.i.* To pick at with the connotation of covertness or secrecy. With the preposition *on*. "If you children don't stop *peefing on* that cake, there'll be none left for dinner." Lancaster County.

peep[1]**:** *n.* The least sandpiper; the western sandpiper; the red-backed sandpiper; the semipalmated sandpiper. S. and C.

peep[2]**:** *n.* A word or other utterance of protest. "Don't let me hear another *peep* out of you."

peep: *v.i.* To voice a protest. "Don't you *peep!*"

pee-pee: *excl.* A call to turkeys. Imitative of the cry of the poults.

peewee: *n.* A small marble. NID, Bart.

penepne [pɪ'nɛpnɪ]: *n.* The hog plum or wild plum of the low country. Origin undetermined.

[4]**persimmon beer:** *n.* A beverage made from ripe persimmons.

[4] A water-tight barrel with eight to ten inches of clear straw or crabgrass hay in the bottom is filled about two-thirds full of ripe persimmons. The straw in the bottom is to prevent the persimmons from clogging the spigot. Water is poured over the persimmons until it does not quite cover them. One should then wait for a few days for the persimmons to "work." The delicious beverage drawn off from a spigot at the bottom of the barrel is one of the products of a culture that seems to be disappearing.

peter bird: *n.* The tufted titmouse. From the bird's cry "Peter, Peter, Peter." S. and C.

pettiauger ['pɛtɪ,ɔgə]: *n.* The *piragua, pirogue*, formerly understood to mean a large freight-carrying cypress dugout, the riverside plantation conveyance. Variant of *piragua*.

pheasant: *n.* The ruffed grouse. NID, S. and C.

piccolo: *n.* An automatic music box, worked by a nickel slot machine. Origin undetermined.

piece: *n.* A familiar or contemptuous reference to a person, usually to girls. "She's a clever little *piece*." "I can't stand that sassy *piece*."

pignut: *n.* See *hickory nut*.

piggin: *n.* A small wooden tub with one of the staves extending a few inches above the rim and used as a handle. Formerly used as a milk pail and called a *milk piggin*. EDD. The *piggin* was sometimes used to carry food to the pigs in the sty, which is a possible origin.

pigpath: *n.* A path made by pigs; a local stop. Contemptuous. "This bus stops at every *pigpath*."

pilch: *n.* A quilted pad used to protect the outer clothes of infants. Cf. NID, Wen.

pinder, pinda: *n.* Peanut. NID, Wen.

pine bark stew: *n.* A fish stew. In pioneer days said to have been served on *pine bark*, which was used as a dish. Another suggested origin arises from the varied contents of such a stew. A typical jocose exchange of remarks is: "Have you put everything into the stew?" "Everything." "*Pine bark* too?" Still another proposal is the general belief that the flavoring is so strong that one could use *pine bark* instead of fish and never know the difference.

piny windy: *n.* The *pride of India*. Negro folk etymology.

piney woods: *n. pl.* Pine forest. Cf. Bart., NID, *piny;* Wen.

pig's ear: *n.* A crudely blatant, vulgar person.

plain avenue: *n.* Private road to a house with no border of trees. Williamsburg County.

Plat Eye: *n.* A malevolent supernatural being who haunts the Black Border in the Georgetown area. See N. G. Gonzales, *The Black Border*.

plenish: *v.t.* To provide, as work stock and implements to operate a farm. Wolfe, NID.

plow-hoe: *n.* A generic name for various forms of plow. Anderson County.

pluffer: *n.* A popgun, made from an elder joint with the pith thrust out, fitted with a plunger not quite the length of the popgun barrel. Green chinaberries are used as ammunition. NID. Scottish and North English dialect.

pluff mud: *n.* The soft, rich, sedimentary mud of the marsh lands in the coastal area. EDD, *pluff,* adj., puffed up, soft, spongy; *pluffy,* adj., soft, porous, spongy.

plumb: *adj.* Exact, accurate. "The likeness is mighty nigh *plumb.*" Wen., NID, Bart.

plumb [plʌm]: *adv.* Quite, entirely, completely. "I'm *plumb* tuckered out." "The bullet went *plumb* through the tree." Wen., NID, Bart.

po-jo: *n.* The heron, the *poor joe.* Gullah. Vai: *podjo.* Turner.

po-jo: *adj.* Drab; dreary; poverty stricken. "Yuh look too *po-jo.*"

poke: *n.* A bag, of paper or other material. Except for the northwest portion of the state, this word is used only in the phrase: "A pig in a *poke.* . ."

pomace ['pʌmɪs]: *n.* 1. The dry pulp of molasses cane or sugar cane after the juice has been pressed out. 2. Apple pulp from the cider press.

pond chicken: *n.* The purple gallinule; the Florida gallinule. S. and C.

pone[1]: *n.* A flat cake, as a pone of corn bread. "A corn *pone.*" Wen.

pone[2]: *n.* A lump, a bump, a swelling. "I hit 'im on the head an' raised a good *pone* over his eye." NID, Wen.

pontop ['pʌn'tɑp]: *prep. upon* the *top* of. On, on top of. "*Pontop* Edisto," on Edisto Island. Gullah.

poodle-doo: *n.* A small bird of the rail family. French: *poule d'eau.* Cooper River region. Cf. Bart.: *pull-doo.*

poor joe: *n.* Same as *po-jo.* For the form, cf. *joe darter, jim dandy, jump-up-johnnie, limber jim,* etc. Wen., NID.

poor mouth, poor mout': *n.* Only in the phrase to "put up *poor mouth,*" to plead poverty; to make a display of one's poverty, helplessness, destitution. Wen.

potato pone: *n.* Grated sweet potato flavored with molasses, milk, spices, cloves, ginger, orange peel, according to taste, cooked and stirred often until thick.

potato pudding: *n.* Same as *potato pone*, except that it has more liquid ingredients and hence a lighter consistency.

potato slip: *n.* When sweet potatoes are planted in a bed, the sprouts growing out of them are called *slips*. These are set out in the potato patch or field. See *mother patch.*

pot pie: *n.* A fruit pie baked in a large, deep pan (formerly a pot) with wheat flour dumplings mixed in with the fruit; a cobbler. Cf. NID: a meat pie boiled in a pot; Bart., *slump.*

pouts: *n. pl.* A fit of pouting. "To have the *pouts.*"

powerhouse: *n.* A bootlegger's shop or place of business. Kingstree.

preacher: *n.* A guide used in making a mark across a board, such as siding, to be sawed, in order to get a perfect fit.

prize: *n.* A lever. NID, *prize*, n. 2.

proud¹: *adj.* Happy, delighted. "I'm mighty *proud* to see you." NID, Wen.

proud²: *adj.* In heat, applied to animals, especially bitches. "A *proud* bitch," also "a *prouding* bitch."

pull-doo: *n.* The salt-marsh hen. Fr. *poule d'eau.* Cf. *poodle-doo.*

pull fodder¹: *v.i.* To give birth to a child. "She is ready to *pull fodder.*" Bamberg County. Origin undetermined.

pull fodder²: *v.t.* To strip the blades from the mature stalk of corn. A handful of such blades is tied into a "hand" which is hung on the stalk. After curing, four or five hands are tied together into a bundle. The practice is on the wane.

pull through: *v.i.* To get well, to recover from illness. Cf. NID, *pull round.*

pull wool: *v.t.* To pluck at a forelock in bowing and scraping, a mode of salutation practiced by slaves. Obsolete.

pulling bone: *n.* The wishbone of a chicken, so called because of the custom of two persons pulling, one on each prong, the one getting the longer piece being the lucky one and supposedly getting his wish fulfilled. Also *pulley bone.*

punching road: *n.* A corduroy road. Probably a variant of *puncheon road.* Cf. NID, *puncheon*, 4.

puntop: *prep.* Same as *pontop.*

purloo, purlo ['pʌrlu, 'pʌrlo]: *n. Pilau.* Wen. *Purloo* may be chicken pilau, shrimp pilau, etc. It always consists, however, of rice cooked with some meat or sea food, and usually well seasoned with black pepper. The word *pilau* is in general use only among the educated.

pursley gut ['pʌslɪ], **pussle gut**: *n.* A large, flabby stomach; one having such a stomach. Sometimes abbreviated to *p. g.* by way of euphemism. *Pursley-gutted*, adj. See Wen. under *pussy-gutted*.

put out: *v.t.* To inconvenience, to cause extra effort of someone. "You sure this won't *put you out?*" Cf. NID, *put out*, f. and i.

put out: *past part adj.* Vexed, angered. "I am plum *put out* with him."

putt [pʌt]: *n.* Turn, in the expression, "It ain't your *putt*." A rebuke to one who speaks or acts out of turn. A possible survival of the Charleston Golf Club of 1793. Charleston.

putten [putn̩]: *past part.* Put. Caused by analogy with strong participles: *given, taken*, etc." He *putten* 'putten,' where he oughta *putten* 'put.' " Georgia.

pyo, py-py ['paɪo, 'paɪ-'paɪ]: *n.* An admonitory and punitive word, meaning a light cuff, a buffet, or a spanking. Coastal nursery usage.

qualified: *past part., adj.* Certain, sure. "I's *qualified* it's so." Negro usage.

quarters: *n. pl.* Negro quarters where the slaves of the plantation lived in one or more rows of cabins. Obsolete. NID.

quile: *v.t.* To coil, same as *kwile*. Cf. *ile* for *oil, bile* for *boil*, etc.

quills: *n. pl.* Pipes of Pan, made by boys from joints of green cane. "Brer Rabbit kin play de *quills* so sweet."—Joel Chandler Harris.

quirl: *n.* A *curl*, as on a watermelon vine. A melon is supposed to be ripe when the *quirl* is dead. Horry County.

rabbit hawk: *n.* Eastern red-tailed hawk, hen hawk, marsh hawk. S. and C.

ractify, rectify: *v.t.* To break, damage or destroy; to overthrow the reason, render insane or *ractified*. Probably an extension of *wreck* or *wrack*.

rain crow: *n.* The yellow-billed cuckoo. NID, S. and C. His note is supposed to foretell rain.

raise: *v.t.* To bring up, rear, train, as a child. Wen.

raised: *past part adj.* Reared, brought up. "I was *raised* to tell the truth."

rattlesnake pilot: *n.* The copperhead. There seems to be no factual basis for the name.

razee: *n.* A drunken spree. Wen.

rearing ['ræɪɪŋ]: *adj.* Eager, keen, anxious, *"Rearing* to go." A horse often rears in his eagerness to begin a race.

reckon: *v.t.* To have or hold an impression, thought, supposition or opinion; hence, to suppose, guess. NID.

redding comb: *n.* A straight comb for untangling, straightening and smoothing the hair, as contrasted with a *back comb, roach comb,* or *side comb,* all of which are worn in the hair, and are more or less ornamental. Cf. *redd,* v.t.

red: *n.* See *brown.*

red-horse bread: *n.* Thick corn meal cakes fried in deep fat in which fish have been fried. Same as *hush puppies, q.v.* Probably named from the *red-horse* fish, with which it was cooked or eaten.

red lane: *n.* The throat. Children's usage. "Down the little *red lane."* Wen., NID.

redd: *v.t.* To clean up, to set in order, as a room, i.e. to make up the bed, to set the furniture in order, to dust, to sweep. Usually followed by the preposition *up.* "*Redd up* the parlor before company comes." Perhaps a shortened form of *ready up,* but I have never heard *ready up* used. NID: *redd-up,* adj., Wen.

reedbird: *n.* The bobolink. NID, S. and C.

remanier [rɪ'menɪə]: *n.* A cobbling tailor who mends clothing. Fr. *remanieur.*

remonie: *n.* Pneumonia. An illiterate corruption.

ricebird: *n.* The bobolink. NID, S. and C.

ride: *v.t.* See under *stake.*

ride the saw: *phr.* To apply one's efforts so that another has to carry the heavier part of the work. From the practice of bearing down on the crosscut saw when one's partner is drawing.

rider: *n.* See under *stake.*

rig: *n.* A half-castrated boar. When one testicle has not come out, it is inaccessible, making complete castration impossible. Hartsville.

rig: *v.t.* To tease, chaff, rally. NID. cf. Wentworth: to run a *rig* on. Obsolescent.

right smart: *n.* A great deal, a large quantity or number; adj., much, many. "How much did it rain?" "Hit rained a *right smart."* *R.S.V.P.* is jocularly interpreted as *"right smart* vittles prepared."

rinsh, rensh: *adj.* Rinsing. "Put some bluing in the last *rinsh* water."

rinsh, rensh: *v.t.* To rinse, as dishes, clothes, etc.

roadwarning: *n.* Notice sent to a male citizen that he is required to work on the public roads in lieu of paying the road tax. The highway system has tended to make this practice obsolete, but it was in use thirty years ago.

robin: *n.* A short coat. Possibly from *robing*, apparel.

rock cake: *n.* A cake of a hard consistency, sold by hawkers on the Charleston waterfront. "*Rock cake* and charlies!" The *charlies* were the familiar gungers or gingerbread.

rogy ['rogɪ]: *adj.* Same as *logy*. Negro usage of coastal area.

roke: *pret.* and *past part.* of *rake.* "I done *roke* up de leaves"; also, *ruck.* Wen.

rookus ['rukəs]: *n.* A row, disturbance, uproar. NID, Wen.

rooster's step: *n.* An indefinite measure of time or distance. "The days are getting a *rooster's step* longer," appreciably longer.

root doctor: *n.* One who heals or pretends to heal by means of medicinal roots and herbs. Cf. *yarbs.*

ro-ro ['roˌro]: *n.* A chimney sweep. So called in Charleston from the sweep's triumphant cry, when emerging from the top of the chimney: "*Ro-ro, ro-ro!*" Obsolete.

rotten [ratn]: *adj.* Spoiled, pampered, especially of children or young people. *Rotten spoiled.*

rotten: *v.t.* To spoil. "You sho' gonna *rotten* dat chile." Mostly Negro usage.

rottening: *pres. part. Rotting*, becoming *rotten.* Wen.

roundabout: *n.* A ball game in which each player successively occupies each position on the team. When a batter is put out, he takes to the field, a fielder takes third base, the third baseman moves to second and so on to first, pitcher, catcher, and batter. At recess schoolboys would storm out of the school house, and the first one to reach the outside shouted: "Roundabout, first strike!" or "Vencha first bat first!" Others followed with a bid for second, catcher, pitcher, etc., and no time was lost in starting a game.

roundance: *n.* See *venture.*

ruction: *n.* An uproar, a state of turbulence, a loud, wordy dispute; a free for all fight. NID, Wen.

ruckus ['rʌkəs, 'rʊkəs]: *n.* Same as *rookus.*

ruin: *v.t.* To deflorate.

ruint: *adj.* Deflorated; *ruined.*

runt: *n.* The smallest pig of a litter. Used of undersized persons in contempt.

runty: *adj.* Of animals or persons: like a runt, undersized.

rurbanism: *n.* A combination of city and country life; dwelling in the country, with perhaps some small farming or trucking interests, and working in the city at regular employment. A blend of *rural* and *urbanism.*

saff-mouthed: *adj.* Flattering. For *salve-mouthed.*

sallet: *n.* Green vegetables, such as mustard, turnip greens, spinach, etc. NID, Wen.

Sally Lum (not to be confused with *Sally Lunn*): *n.* Skimmings from jelly while in the process of boiling. Origin undetermined.

salt: *n.* Seashore or tidewater region. "To live on the *salt.*"

sandchicken: *n.* The least sandpiper; the sanderling; the redbacked sandpiper; the semipalmated sandpiper. S. and C.

sand lugs: *n. pl.* Lowest grade of tobacco leaves, growing low on the plant, and having sand beaten upon them by rains.

sand martin: *n.* The rough-winged swallow. S. and C.

Sarahgodlin, Sallygodlin: *adj.* Same as *antigodlin*, *q.v.* Apparently these variants arise from a mistaken understanding of *antigodlin*, as if it were *aunty-godlin.*

sass: *n.* 1. Impudent or impertinent talk, especially of a younger to an older person, an inferior to a superior. 2. Garden *sass*, vegetables, especially green vegetables. Wen. Cf. Bart., *sauce.*

sassafrass tea, sassifax tea: *n.* A tea made from the dried roots of the *sassafras.*

save all: *n.* Same as *scramlins.*

scaly bark: *n.* See *hickory nut.*

scare up: *v.t.* To collect on the spur of the moment, to make an impromptu collection and preparation. "If you will stay, my wife will *scare up* some supper in a jiffy."

scavenger cart: *n.* A garbageman's cart. Now obsolescent, since the coming of the truck.

schneiders: *n. pl.* Dumplings. Chicken *schneiders* are made by rolling the biscuit dough out thin, cutting it into slivers and dropping these into the pot in which the chicken is being stewed. Lexington County and Dutch Fork. This dish is called *chicken dumplings* or *chicken stew* in Abbeville, Greenwood and McCormick counties. Ger. *schneiden*, to cut.

scramlins: *n. pl.* Corn meal cooked in the liquid in which liver pudding has been cooked. Probably from NID, *scramble,* v.t. 4.

scrouge [skraʊdʒ]: *v.t.* and *v.i.* To crowd; to press one's way into a crowded seat or standing room. Probably from *crowd.* For the change of *-d* to *-dge,* cf. *toadgefrog.* EDD has *scrouge, scrudge, crudge* with the same general meaning. NID, Wen.

scrounge [skraʊndʒ]: *v.t.* and *v.i.* 1. Variant of *scrouge.* 2. To forage for food; to obtain a meal by devious ways.

scrunch [skrʌntʃ]: *v.i.* and *v.t.* To crouch or stoop down. Usually with *down;* to crush, crunch, break to pieces or flatten under pressure. NID, Wen.

scusin: *prep.* Except, excepting, not counting. From *excusing.* "Dinner is ready *scusin* de coffee." NID, *excusing.*

seadog: *n.* 1. The black skimmer, shearwater. 2. A drink composed of rum, maple syrup, lemon juice and water. S. and C.

segaciate, segashiate [sɪˈɡæʃɪet.]: *v.i.* In the jocular greeting: "How is your corporosity *segaciating*?" meaning, how is your health? See *corporosity.*

set: *v.i.* To sit.

set up to: *v.t.* To court, spark, woo.

settin' gum: *n.* A place arranged to set hens to brood. Probably on the analogy of *bee gum.*

shadbelly: *n.* A long, broad crosscut saw. So called on account of its shape. Cf. NID.

shadow soup: *n.* Thin, watery soup.

shame: *adj.* Ashamed. "Be *shame* of yourself." Wen.

shamey flower: *n.* The opopanax, so called because sensitive.

shed: *adj.* Same as *shut,* q.v. Wen.

shed room: *n.* A shed, a lean-to. A shed room is usually built on the side of the barn, but may also be built against the dwelling. Wen.

sheep dung tea: *n.* A homemade prescription, made with the natural pills found in a sheep pasture. By way of euphemism the remedy was called *sheep suet.* Supposed to cure the measles, or to "bring out" the measles.

sheep shaffle: *n.* Same as *sheep dung tea.*

shell out: *v.i.* and *v.t.* To pay. "If you want this you'll have to *shell out.*" "I had to *shell out* two bucks for it." Cf. Wen.

shet: *adj.* Same as *shut,* q.v. Wen.

shikepoke: *n.* The shitepoke. Wen.

shirttail: *n.* The red-headed woodpecker. So called because of white feathers on wings and under parts.

shirttail bird: *n.* The red-headed woodpecker. S. and C.

shirttail boy: *n.* Any adolescent or younger boy. Wen. Such boys often "go in their *shirttail*," wear only a shirt.

shoe bread: *n.* A thin sandwich of bread and bacon, slipped into the heel of one's shoe, to entice a desirable dog away from his master's home.

shoo-fly: *n.* A railway train on a small branch line. Also a passenger car attached to a freight train. Probably so called because of its short flight, like a fly that has been *shooed.* Cf. NID, Wen.

shool [ʃul]: *v.i.* To drag the feet in walking; to walk with a shuffle. NID, cf. Wen.: *shool*, to saunter.

short sweetening: *n.* Sugar, used as sweetening in coffee, tea, etc., or in cooking. NID, Wen.

shrimp plate: *n.* A measure (plate full) of shrimp with the heads still on. Charleston. Obsolete.

shulalay ['ʃulə,le]: *n.* A celebration formerly held on the Battery at Charleston, S. C., by the Negroes on July Fourth. The Battery was turned over to the Negroes for the day. Songs and dancing were featured. Some remember this celebration under the name *too-la-loo.* One of the songs went:

> Alligator motion, too-la-loo,
> Mighty pretty motion, too-la-loo.

shut: *adj. past part.* Rid. To be or get *shut* of. Cf. Prov. Eng. *shuttance*, riddance. For *shet* cf. dialect variants such as *tech* for *touch. Shed* may be reminiscent of the verb *shed*, or may be a participle of this verb. Wen.

sidegadling ['saɪd,gædlɪŋ]: *adj.* Awry, askew; off the main track. Applied to a path which wanders aimlessly from the main track. Cf. *gadling*, adj., wandering, *gadling*, n. a vagabond. Cf. *antigodlin*, etc.

sidegodlin ['saɪd,gɑdlɪn]: *adj.* Same as *sidegadling.*

side meat: *n.* Salt pork sides with one or more streaks of lean meat. NID.

sifer: *n.* See under *heabe.*

sillybub: *n.* Sweet milk flavored with sherry wine, whipped into a frothy drink. Cf. Wen., and NID: *sillabub.*

simlin: *n.* 1. A very small helping or portion of food. 2. A semblance, a resemblance. "Brudduh, you ain' hardly a *simlin* of yo' natchul self." Said after a severe illness or other cause of physical decline. *Simlin* is a corruption of *resemblance.* Negro usage, Pee Dee.

singeing: *adv.* Very, intensely, exceedingly, in the expression: "*Singeing* cold," cf. *swingeing.* Vegetation appears to have been scorched or *singed* after such cold.

sit up: *v.i.* To hold a wake with a dead body. The custom is dying out.

situate: *adj.* Accustomed, adjusted, used. "I ent see she, but she see me 'cause she eye *situate* to de da'k," that is, her eyes were used to the darkness. Negro, coastal usage.

sivvy bean: *n.* *Sieva* bean. Originating in Charleston, this form has come into use in other parts of the state. "From the *Seewee* Indians. Many Charlestonians pronounce it *seewee* bean." Chapman Milling. *Sewee* bay, whence the seed came is also suggested as the origin.

skiddler: *n.* Black mallard, black duck. S. and C.

skimption: *n.* A very small amount, a smidgin. Wen.

skin by: *v.i.* To qualify on the narrowest margin, with the minimum performance. NID, *skin through.*

skins: *n. pl.* The small intestines of hogs, cleaned and used for stuffing sausage. A euphemistic evasion of the word *guts.*

skylark: *v.i.* To go courting; to flirt. "To go *skylarking*," "to *skylark* around," etc. Cf. NID. Obsolescent.

sleep in: *v.i.* 1. To cut class. College usage. 2. Of maidservants, to sleep in the house where they are employed.

sling: *n.* A long-handled shovel.

slipe: *v.t.* To sideswipe. Cf. Wen. Possibly a blend of *slice* and *swipe* or some such combination.

slow poke: *n.* NID, *poke*, n. "A lazy person." Appears in S. C., as far as has been ascertained, only in the combination, *slow poke.*

sluts wool: *n.* Same as *house moss, q.v.*

sly: *adv.* Sneaking. Only of cold weather. "It's *sly* cold."

smarts: *n. pl.* Ostentatious, exuberant display of oneself; showing off. Only in the expressions: "to have the *smarts*," "to have a (bad) case of *smarts*." Usually but not always of children. "He's got the *smarts* so bad he can't see straight."

smidgen, smidgin: *n.* A very small amount. NID, Wen.

smithereens: *n. pl.* Small fragments of anything broken. EDD.

Cf. EDD, *smither*, fragments, atoms, slivers; *smeddum*, the powder or finest part of ground malt; *smiddum*, ore which passes through a sieve..., powdered lead ore.

snake doctor: *n.* A mosquito hawk, dragon fly. Upper S. C. The dragon fly is usually seen near small streams where it deposits its eggs. Near such small streams water moccasins are frequently seen. This association may account for the name.

snapper: *n.* A civilian foreman on a government (military or naval) project. Origin undetermined.

snib: *n.* A foul ball.

snib: *v.t.* To touch lightly.

snide: *adj.* Mean, underhanded; "a *snide* trick;" cutting, malicious; "a *snide* remark." O.E. *snithan*, to cut; EDD, *snithe*, to cut. Cf. NID.

sniff: *n.* A small swallow or drink of whiskey.

sniggle: *v.i.* To snicker; to laugh foolishly. May be a blend of *snicker* and *giggle*. NID.

snither [snɪðə]: *adj.* Sharp, cutting, usually in the phrase "a *snither* wind." Cf. *snide*, EDD *snitherin*, pres. part. adj., sharp and keen.

snolly-goggle: *n.* A naughty boy. Cf. Wen., *snolly-goster*, a shyster.

snorf [snɔrf]: *n.* Same as *house-moss*, *q.v.* Origin undetermined.

snuck [snʌk]: *v.i. Past tense* and *past part.* of *sneak*.

sont [sɑnt]: *v.t. Past tense* and *past part.* of *send*. "Yo' pa *sont* for you." Wen.

sooey: *interj.* Used to frighten hogs out of one's way. In some sections of lower S. C., used to call hogs to the trough for slops, etc. Cf. NID, Wen. See also *hooey*.

sooky ['sʊkɪ]: *n.* A call to cattle. "*Sooky, sooky, sook* cow!" Upcountry. Cf. NID, Wen.

sookin ['sʊkɪn]: *n.* A bag, usually of burlap. Union County and environs.

sootlin ['sʊtlɪn] **ball:** *n.* A very dirty child. Apparently connected with *soot*. However, cf. EDD, *suddle*, to soil, to defile, n., a stain.

sot: *adj., past tense* and *past part.* Set. "He is *sot* in his ways." "I *sot* the hen."

sotay [ˌsoˈte]: *adv.* Exceedingly, extremely. "Hot *sotay*," "cold *sotay*," very hot, very cold. Negro dialect. Darlington. Obsolete (?).

soup bunch: *n.* A variety of vegetables tied up in a bunch to be used for making soup.

souse: *n.* The edible parts of the head and feet of a hog, cut up fine, cooked together, and seasoned. When allowed to cool, it forms a gelatinous cake. Same as *hog head cheese.* Cf. Wen.

spark: *n.* A sweetheart. Cf. Wen., *spark,* v.

spark: *v.t.* and *v.i.* To go courting, to court, woo. NID, Wen., Bart.

sparrowgrass: *n.* From *asparagus.* Also, *grass.* Wen., NID.

spiketail: *n.* The ruddy duck. NID, S. and C.

spit limit: *n.* The limit of time allotted for an errand. The sender *spits* on the floor. The messenger is supposed to deliver the message or run the errand and return before the spit dries.

spittin' image: *n.* Spit and image. A corruption. *Spit and image* became first *spit 'n' image,* which was then "improved" to *spitting image.* All these forms are heard. NID, Wen.

spooner: *n.* A hearty eater. An active wielder of the spoon. "Joe, why do you buy so much rations?" "Well, I tell you Cap'n, I's got six head in my house an' ev'y Gawd's one kin lif' a hebby *spoon.*"

spotty: *n.* The spotted sandpiper. S. and C.

spread: *v. refl.* To go to great length in entertaining; to expand one's activities. Cf. Bart.

sprig, sprigtail: *n.* The pintail duck. S. and C.

square: *n.* The three-sided bud of the cotton blossom. Wen. Origin undetermined.

squeedunk: *n.* A device of the practical joker consisting of a long nail whose point is fixed under the weatherboarding on the outside of a house, and a long string fastened to the head of the nail. The practical joker at the other end of the string at a safe distance pulls the string taut, then draws a piece of rosin or beeswax along the string, producing thus an outlandish noise inside of the house.

squinch owl: *n.* Screech owl. Wen. Var. *scrooch owl.*

stable surf: *n.* Stable manure. See *surf.* Horry County.

stake: *n.* In rail fence construction, one of the two rails or stakes leaned up, one in each of the opposite outside angles at each corner. These rails then cross above the fence, and another rail, called a *rider,* is laid in the crotches thus formed, making the fence much higher. The process is called *staking and riding* the fence. Cr. Bart. and Wen., *stake and rider*.

stake: *v.t.* See *stake*, n.

stand: *v.i.* To be, to exist, to appear. "Boy, how de sky *stan'*?" "De sky *stan'* blue." "How you *stan'*, ol' man?" "Dem oranges *stan'* rotten." Negro usage.

standbacks: *n. pl.* Same as *studs*.

stantion: *n.* An appointed station on board a boat. "Hold your *stantion!*" that is, keep your place. John Bennett suggests the Spanish *estancia* as a probable origin.

stave: *v.i.* To run, to go in a hurry. "He went *staving* down the road." NID, Wen.

stick-in-the-mud: *n.* 1. A familiar, jocular nickname. "How's the old *stick-in-the-mud?*" 2. A person set in his ways; reluctant to act or change; reactionary.

stink: *v.t.* To give a (pleasant) flavor or savor to. "You ain't got enough fish to *stink* the pan." Anglo-Saxon *stincan* meant to have an odor.

stinkbird: *n.* The eastern Savannah sparrow. S. and C.

stocking legs: *n. pl.* Legs of a colored horse, white from the knee down.

stone curlew: *n.* The eastern willet. NID, S. and C.

stoop crops: *n. pl.* "Crops that require much labor in which the workers *stoop* down to produce. . . ." L. S. Wolfe, *Farm Glossary*.

stoopie: *n.* A hunchback. Horry County.

stove up: *past part. adj.* Worn out from exertion; stiff in the joints; sore from exercise; especially unwonted exercise. Possibly from NID *stave*, v.t. 4, to beat or cudgel; to knock.

stranger's fever: *n.* Yellow fever. *Strangers*, having developed no immunity, were more susceptible to attack.

streak o' lean: *n.* Salt pork sides with one or more streaks of lean meat.

string: *v.i.* To go along with, and take part in an enterprise, plan, etc. "We'll *string* along with you." Cf. NID, *string*, intr., 2.

strip: *v.i.* To change clothes. Horry County.

stuck: *adj. past part.* Said of a young pair at a party when they have exhausted all topics of conversation and begin to feel embarrassed, or in dancing, when they are never broken.

studs: *n. pl.* A show of temper in a horse, wherein he refuses to move. A horse is said to have the *studs*, or to take the *studs* or *standbacks*.

stump: *v.t.* To stub, as to *stump* one's foot or toe. Wen. Originally this probably meant "to strike against a *stump*.

stumphole liquor: *n.* Same as *stumpwater*.

stumpwater: *n.* 1. Illicit liquor, boot-leg liquor. 2. Water from a *stumphole*, used by those too improvident to dig a well.

stymie: *v.t.* To frustrate; to block the plans of; to hem in.

succa ['sʌkə]: *adj.* Same as; just like. Gonz., *sukkuh*.

sugar biscuit: *n.* A cookie. These seldom form a part of a regular meal, but are intended to be eaten between meals, mostly for children. Charleston and environs.

sugar house: *n.* A place where slaves were sent to be lashed, then dipped in brine to prevent soreness. Obsolete.

sugar teat: *n.* A pacifier, formed by tying a small quantity of sugar up in a cloth. In Horry County butter is added. In Newberry they dip the sugar teat in cream to prime it.

suggins: *n. pl.* Wraps, such as cloaks, shawls, scarfs, etc. "Get your *suggins* together and let's go." Cf. NID and Wen., *sugan*.

sulk: *v.i.* Of horses and oxen, to refuse to rise from a lying position; in a sullen mood.

sulks: *n. pl.* A sulky mood. "To be in the *sulks*," or "to have the *sulks*."

summer duck: *n.* The wood duck, acorn duck. S. and C.

suption: *n.* 1. Substance, as applied to food. "The yellow corn has more *suption* in it." 2. The rich juice or gravy from cooked meat; the drippings from a roast fowl or beef. Probably a corruption of *substance*. Variants: *suction, substish*.

surf: *n.* A mixture of rich soil and leaves. Mr. M. A. Wright suggests that this is from *surface* earth. Horry County.

surf gull: *n.* Bonaparte's gull. S. and C.

swage: *v.t.* and *v.i.* To reduce a swelling; to become reduced. EDD. From *assuage*.

swage: *v.t.* To strip a milch cow. *Swaging* or stripping is done with a different motion from that of ordinary milking. In stripping or *swaging* the thumb and forefinger are drawn with pressure down the teat.

swampreed: *n.* Rice. Wen.

sweet monkey: *n.* A potent mixture of rum and sorghum molasses.

sweet-mouth: *v.t.* To flatter. "You jes' *sweet-mouthin'* me."

sweet-mouthed: *adj.* Flattering, ingratiating. Wen.

sweet tooth: *n.* An appetite for sweets, as desserts, candies, etc.

swidget: *n.* A fit of anxious, fidgety nervousness.

swidget: *v.i.* To move about, gesticulate in a peevish, nervous, fidgety manner. Apparently a blend of *swivet, q.v.* and *fidget.*

swigger: *v.i.* A euphemism for *swear;* "Well, I'll *swigger!*" Also "I'll be *swiggered!*" Expression of mild surprise. Wen.

swinge cat: *n.* A stray, ownerless street-and-alley cat, ill-fed, lean and scabby. Applied in derogatory humor to any wretched animal or human, ragged, gray-complexioned and forlorn. Charleston.

swinger ['swɪndʒə]: *n.* A very cold day. Same as *brinjer.* Lower S. C. See *singeing.*

swinging ['swɪndʒɪn]: *adj.* Very cold. Lower S. C.

swivet: *n.* A state of agitation, frantic confusion, usually connected with the idea of haste. NID, Wen.

tacky: *adj.* Grotesque; outmoded; cheaply pretentious in dress. In the expression *tacky party* most usual, but also used to designate one's appearance, especially in clothing. NID, Wen.

tail: *v.t.* See under *handstick.*

talk turkey: *v.i.* To talk straight to the point, plainly, clearly; to come to the point; to talk sense. "Now you are *talking turkey.*" Cf. NID.

tanky bag: *n.* A bag formerly carried by colored retainers when visiting former slave owners, shortly after the end of slavery. The *tanky bag* was filled and the bearers expressed their thanks: "*Tanky, tanky,*" whence the name. Cf. *PADS*, 13, p. 10, *thanky-bag.*

tarrigate ['tærɪˌget]: *v.t.* Interrogate; to vex, to pester. Low country Negro usage. "Mule stop, 'cause mule know yuh haffa *tarrigate* pusson een de road".

task: *n.* 1. A stint of work for a field laborer, especially a hoehand; in the rice field, a quarter-acre; in the corn or cotton field, a half-acre. 2. Hence a measure of distance (about 100 ft.). A shotgun will be said "to throw two *tas'* and kill." Charleston. Cf. NID.

tater: *n.* Potato.

teacake: *n.* A cookie; a thin, flat sweetcake, made for children, to be eaten between meals; has little to do with afternoon tea. Same as *sugar biscuit.*

tease: *v.t.* In picking cotton, to pick carelessly, leaving part of the locks in the burr.

tech: *v.t.* To *touch.* Wen.

teched: *past part. Touched,* slightly unbalanced mentally.

tech-me-not: *n. Touch-me-not,* the garden balsam. So called because the seed pods at a certain stage burst open on contact. Upcountry and mountain usage.

telltale snipe: *n.* The greater yellowlegs; the lesser yellowlegs. S. and C.

tender: *adj.* Weak, fragile, as a *tender* board, a *tender* bridge. A sailboat which capsizes easily is described as *tender.* Conway, Charleston.

tetter: *n.* Potato. Gullah.

thataway: *adv. That way.* Adverb of direction or manner. "He went *thataway,*" "Don't do it *thataway.*" Wen.

theglin: *n.* A powerful concoction of fermented honey, water, and sometimes yeast; *metheglin.* Said to be still produced in the high Appalachians. Sometimes called *metzeglin.*

them: *pron.* Same as *those.*

thisaway: *adv. This way.* Adverb of direction or manner. "He went *thisaway.*" "Do it *thisaway.*" Other forms are *this here way, this here away.* Wen.

those: *pron.* The others, especially others of a family or group. "I saw Mr. Smith and *those* at church today," meaning Mr. Smith and the others of his family. In the low country the Negroes say: "Mr. Smith *dem.*" Usage of lower S. C. Cf. *and those, PADS,* 2, p. 39.

tick-tack: *n.* A device for playing practical jokes, consisting of a small weight hung by a string over a window on the outside, worked from a safe distance by pulling and releasing a string attached to the weight, thus causing it to strike against the window. Cf. *squeedunk.* NID, EDD.

tief: *v.t.* To steal: "tief paat [tif pæ:t]," to sneak away, that is, "steal a path." Coastal Negro usage.

ting an' ting: *adj. Thing and thing.* The same; exactly alike. Coastal Negro usage. "Dem two chillun is *ting and ting.*"

tippet: *n.* A short cape. Cf. NID, *tippet,* n. 2.

title: *n.* A name. Negro usage.

titty: *n.* 1. Milk from the breast. Child's speech. 2. *pl.* The female breasts. NID.

tizzy: *n.* A state of confusion, hurry, disturbance, nervous uncertainty. Wen.

toadge frog: *n.* A toad. For the change: *d:dge,* compare *todes: todge,* for *towards.*

tote: *v.t.* To carry. Gullah. Belgian Congo: *tota,* to pick up. Turner, NID, Wen., Bart.

todes, todge [todz, todʒ]: *prep. Towards,* in the direction of. "He went off *todge* home."

tommytoe ['tɑmɪˌto]: *n.* A small variety of tomato.

tompee, tompy: *n.* A sweetmeat. Origin undetermined.

tomtit: *n.* The tufted titmouse; Worthington's marsh wren. S. and C. Cf. NID.

tom-walkers: *n. pl.* Stilts. Children's usage.

ton timber: *n.* Extra large, long timber, especially pine. *Timber* refers to wood on the stump or in the log. Lumber section, coastal area.

too-la-loo: *n.* See *Shulalay.*

tosey: *n.* 1. An affectionate name for a *toad.* An old Scottish usage. Cf. *toadge frog.* 2. A she-dog. 3. A woman.

tother: *pron.* The other. *Adj.,* the other, as *"tother* day." *Tother* is never preceded by an article, as the initial *t* represents the article.

touchous: *adj.* Touchy, sensitive, easily offended. NID. "He's *touchous* about his health."

trade: *n.* Compliment. "I have a good *trade* for you." Usually in the phrase *last-go-trade,* whereby the speaker demands a compliment in prepayment. Confined mostly to teen-agers. Wen., *trade-last.*

traipse [treps]: *v.i.* To go, especially to walk about aimlessly, idly, to gad about, usually with the prep. *about, around.* Of animals as well as people. "There goes old Sook *traipsing* off again." NID, Wen.

trash mover: *n.* 1. A heavy downpour of rain. 2. An energetic, hustling person, a "go-getter."

treadfast: *n.* The nettle-like, prickly leafage of the wild potato. "To walk as if he had *treadfast* under his feet," to walk quickly, lightly, gingerly.

treadsalve ['trɛdsæːv]: *n.* The sand-bur; the North American nightshade, (tread softly). Wen. Cf. *PADS*, 13, p. 10, *tread saft.*

trus'-me-Gawd: *n.* That is, *I trust my God*—a small canoe or small boat; a small dugout. Negro usage of S. C. coastal area.

trussle: *n.* 1. The threshold. Apparently a corruption of *threshold.* 2. A *trestle.*

tubby: *adj.* Fat, corpulent. Only of persons.

tunnel bed: *n.* A trundle bed. Corruption of *trundle* bed.

turkey bumps: *n. pl.* Goose-flesh.

turkey's nest: *n.* Same as *house-moss, q.v.*

turn: *n.* A quantity of grain carried to the mill for grinding; the flour or meal brought home from the mill. NID, Wen., Bart.

turn flour: *n.* Corn meal. So called because originally the corn was taken to the mill and the *turn* of meal brought back. Coastal Negro pronunciation, *"tu'n flour." PADS*, 5, p. 42, *turn* of corn.

turtledove: *n.* The eastern mourning dove. S. and C.

twine: *n.* A strong flavor, a tang, a twang. Probably a corruption of *twang.* "That blackberry acid's got a *twine* to it."

twitch: *v.t.* To keep a horse or mule quiet and still by means of a *twitch,* to use a *twitch* on. Cf. NID, *twitch,* n. 4.

'twixt: *prep.* Betwixt. *"Twixt* the devil and the deep blue sea."

twixt-hell-and-the-whiteoak: *n.* The chuck-will's-widow. Onomatopoetic. A close imitation of the bird's notes. S. and C.

two eaty: *n.* Same as *ninny,* 1.

two-headed: *adj.:* Having a depression running across the head from one side to the other, as if the head were partly divided into two sections.

two-time, double-time: *v.t.* To deceive, cheat; to practice duplicity, double dealing on a person. Possibly formed on the pattern of the double deal. *Two-timer, n. two-timing, adj.*

twofer: *n.* A cheap cigar, selling *two for* a nickel.

unbeholdenst: *adj.* Unseen; unobligated.

unbeknownst: *adj.* Unknown. NID, Wen.

unders: *n. pl.* In wrestling, boys begin by taking hold of each other around the chest, each passing his right arm under the other's left or vice-versa. A contestant who is allowed to put both his arms under the arms of his opponent has all *unders* a great advantage. "I kin give you *all unders* and throw you down."

ungodly: *adv.* Extremely. "Ole Miss Lou bin dat *ungodly* kind to we." Also in an unpleasant sense: "It's *ungodly* cold."

unh-hunh, hunh-unh [ˈʔʌ̃ˈhʌ̃, ˈhʌ̃ˈʔʌ̃]: Affirmation and negation respectively. These sounds are made with lips either parted or closed. See *hah-ah*. In each case the accent falls ordinarily with equal force on both syllables. However, great variety of expression is achieved by a variation in accent and tone.

up and about: *adj.* In good health, able to follow one's normal course of life. This is usually said of one who has been ill or otherwise disabled.

uppity: *adj.* Pretentious, snobbish, impudent.

use: *v.i.* To conjure, work a cure by magic, e.g. to *use for fire* means to heal a burn by passing the hands over the burned place and pronouncing certain magic words. Dutch Fork. Cf. Wen., *try for*.

venture: *interj.* In playing marbles, used to prevent one's opponent from taking advantage of some rule of the game. *"Venture roundance!"* pronounced by an opponent deprives the player from moving in an arc around his target for a better shot. The player can retain his right to roundance by saying: "Roundance no lose." If he fails to add the last two words, his opponent may by saying "lose two yards" force him to withdraw that distance before he shoots. Cf. NID, *fen*.

wampus [ˈwɔmpəs]: *n.* An imaginary sea monster. "To catch a *wampus*." Cf. NID, Wen.

wampus cat [ˈwɔmpəskæt]: *n.* A mythical green-eyed cat, having occult powers.

wampus-jawed: *adj.* Having a swollen jaw.

wang: *n.* A peculiar, unusual savor or flavor in food, especially in meats. A tinge, a tang, a twang. "This beef has a *wang* to it."

warning paper: *n.* A paper with black ribbon attached, bearing the names of friends and neighbors to whom it is carried, announcing a death and the time and place of the funeral.

washing: *n.* Bathing; swimming. "To go in *washing*, or *awashing*." Wen.

washhole: *n.* Swimming hole, especially a broad, deep place in a stream used for swimming.

Washington pie: *n.* A kind of baker's "hash," made up of leftovers, sweetened, baked and sold in rectangular slices; also called *down balance*, owing to its solidity. No one but a growing boy could digest it. Obsolescent (?).

wasp nest, was' nes': *n.* Ordinary baker's bread, so called because of its insubstantial, porous structure; state wide. A small loaf, pierced with finger thrusts, with molasses poured into the openings. Florence. From Charleston: A small loaf with a pointed end scooped out and filled with molasses. Another prescription is to take the end of a loaf, scoop out the crumb, pour the molasses in and replace the crumb. *Was' nes'* will dull the keenest appetite in short order. See *molasses biscuit.*

watersilk: *n.* Same as *frog spittle* and *frogum, qq.v.*

waysy: *adj.* Addicted to pronouncedly aggressive or disagreeable *ways* of speech or action.

wear: *v.t.* Followed by the prep. *out.* To beat, to thrash, to whip, but only of children by way of correction. "If you don't bring in that stove-wood, I'm going to *wear* you *out!*" Wen.

weatherwiser: *n.* A weather prophet. Lower Richland County.

wet: *v.t.* and *v.i.* To make water. "Back in my day the teacher used to thrash us till we *wet.*" "To *wet* the bed."

wham: *v.t.* and *v.i.* To strike with a loud noise, to bang, to beat with resonant blows; to throw a thing against some object so as to cause a loud noise. Cf. *whang, bang.* This may be a blend of *whang* and *slam.* NID.

whampsy-jawed ['hwɔmpsɪ]: *adj.* Having large or full jaws. Cf. *wampus-jawed.*

whang: *interj.* An exclamation expressing a blow or impact accompanied by a loud noise. Also used adverbially. "The car went *whang* into a lamp post." NID.

whang: *v.t.* and *v.i.* To strike with a resounding noise, to wham. NID.

whangdoodle: *n.* An imaginary creature. To express the idea that a person has entirely disappeared, with a connotation of flight from the law, it is said: "He is gone where the woodbine twineth, and the *whangdoodle* mourns for his long lost love." NID, Wen. Spartanburg and Columbia. Also Georgia and Charleston.

What for: *phr.* In the questions, "*What for a* time did you have?" "*What for a* day is it?" "*What for a* horse is he?" EDD, Vol II, p. 452. "*What* is he *for* a fool that betroths himself to unquietness?" *Much Ado About Nothing,* I, iii, 59. This is compared in NID and by Kittredge, *Sixteen Plays of Skakespeare,* p. 116, with the German *was für ein.* The comparisons made are probably not intended to indicate any borrowing, however. The dialect usage here cited survives among the English stock of the mountains and foothills of North and South Carolina who have never come under any German influence. NID.

whelp: *n.* A wale or welt on the skin caused by a stripe or blow; any raised place on skin or flesh caused by a blow, an insect bite or the like. Wen. Common in upper S. C. and in Horry Co. Excrescent *h:* welt, *whelt,* and by folk etymology, *whelp.*

whetrock: *n.* A small whetstone used by boys for sharpening pocketknives.

whicker: *v.i.* To neigh; to whinny. NID, Wen.

whiff: *n.* A small drink of whiskey. Cf. *sniff.* See NID, *whiff,* v. 3; n. 4, b.

whipstitch: *n.* A trick, dodge, artifice. "He took advantage of every *whipstitch* to win." Cf. Wen.

white side meat: *n.* Salt pork sides with one or more streaks of lean meat. Same as *streak o' lean,* and *side meat.*

whosomever room: *n.* The guest room. Santee.

whuffuh ['hwʌfə]: *adv. What for;* why.

whup [hwʊp]: *v.t.* To *whip.* NID, Wen.

whuppin', whupping, ['hwʊpɪn]: *n.* A *whipping.*

whut [hwʌt]: *pron. What.* Especially in an unaccented position. This pronunciation is quite general, and is even heard from the platform in a formal address. The exclamatory: "What?" is more apt to have the standard pronunciation.

wild canary: *n.* The yellow warbler; the eastern goldfinch. NID, S. and C.

will-willet: *n.* The eastern willet. NID, S. and C.

wire-work: *v.t.* and *v.i.* To plot, scheme, plan slyly. "He is *wire-working* to dodge the issue." "He *wire-worked* his plans to suit the occasion."

witch: *n.* Same as *preacher.*

witch water: *n.* Mirage seen on hard-surface roads in summer. Low Country Negro dialect.

won't *v.i. Wa'n't,* contraction of *was* + *not.* Wasn't, weren't. "That was the way of it, *won't* it?" "We *won't* there when it happened."

wood burner: *n.* A name given by Negroes to a slow, uninteresting preacher. Cf. *coal burner.* Obsolescent.

woodcock: *n.* The southern pileated woodpecker. S. and C. Cf. NID.

woods colt: *n.* An illegitimate child.

yaller belly: *n.* See *yellow belly.*

yank: *v.t.* To jerk roughly; of persons, to jerk, pull suddenly and rudely. "To *yank* a person out of bed." NID.

yarbs: *n. pl.* Medicinal herbs; "knowing yarbs" means having particular power to heal, with the implication of occult knowledge or cunning. Wen. Cf. NID, *yerba.*

yard axe [jɑːd æks]: *n.* A preacher of little ability. Negro usage. The *yard axe* is used in many ways by many hands, and cannot be kept sharp.

yard axe lawyer: *n.* A person, not a lawyer, who nevertheless gives legal opinions on a variety of subjects. Cf. *yard axe.*

yard child: *n.* 1. A child old and mature enough to shift for himself in the yard. 2. A legitimate child; *yard chillun.*

yard comb: *n.* A rake. Santee river.

yard egg: *n.* An egg of the highest quality and freshness. So called because produced on the premises.

yard-name: *n.* Nickname. Horry County.

yarsbob: *n. pl. Earbobs.* Low country Negro usage.

yearbobs: *n. pl. Earbobs.*

yeddy: *v.t.* To hear. Gonz.

yellow belly, yaller belly: *n.* A Negro. A term of reproach.

yellowhammer: *n.* The southern flicker. S. and C.

yinner, yunner, yunna ['jɪnə, 'jʌnə, 'jʌnə]: *pron. You all.* Gullah.

hi-yi ['haɪ'jaɪ]: *interj.* An exclamation of disgust, disapproval. Gullah.

yon: *demonstr. adj.* Yonder. Designates what lies at some distance.

yon side: *prep.* On the other side of. *"Yon side* the river."

youngun: *n.* Young one, that is, a child. Also of young animals, especially new-born: "The cat got six *younguns."* Wen.

zebra woodpecker: *n.* The red-bellied woodpecker. S. and C.

EXPRESSIONS FROM RURAL FLORIDA

LUCILLE AYERS, MRS. HAZEL MCLAUGHLIN,
MRS. ROY MOBLEY, FOSTER OLROYD

The words in this list and the Minorcan list, which follows, were collected by the persons named above and by Miss Friedman. They were students at the University of Florida during the summer of 1949 in Ernest H. Cox's English 306. The work was done at the suggestion of and under the guidance of Mr. Cox, who edited the lists.—The Editor

A. GLOSSARY

ankle-hanger: *n.* Evening dress. Backwoods dialect of Suwannee River area.

bamboo vine: *n.* The smilax, the tender tips of which are cooked and eaten for greens.

bar-head: *n.* A horse that cannot be trained to work or to be ridden. Cowboy speech.

bedded-down: *adj.* When animals and riders stop for rest at night, the cattle are said to be bedded-down.

belly-breakers: *n.* The large biscuits served by cooks in cow-camps.

big 'uns: *n.* The large biscuits served by cooks in cow-camps.

breaking corn: *phr.* Taking the ear of corn from the stalk.

bronc-stomping, bronk-stomping: *n.* Breaking horses. Cowboy speech.

bunch: *n.* Family. "Sarah's *bunch.*"

bunkers: *n.* Fish which do not sell in the market for food, but which do sell for catfish bait.

cabbage, cabbage-tree: *n.* The palmetto palm.

cabbage bitter: *n.* The tender part of the palmetto leaf, just below the bud.

cabbage boot: *n.* The part of the palmetto leaf which is attached to the tree.

cabbage log: *n.* A palmetto log.

cabbage stalk: *n.* The stem of the palmetto palm leaf.

cabbage woods: *n.* Areas in which the palmetto is practically the only tree growing.

caflummoxed on the job: *phr.* Failed at a task. Hernando County.

camp-horse: *n.* A horse staked near the place where the cow-puncher bunks at night.

camp-wagon: *n.* A supply vehicle, formerly a horse-drawn wagon, now commonly a truck. Cowboy speech.

cattle-drivin' horse: *n.* A horse especially trained to round up and bring back to the herd cattle which wander away.

circle-buckin': *phr.* The manner in which a horse sometimes bucks, staying in a circle of about fifteen feet in diameter.

coat-tails poppin': *phr.* Description of a person in an angry hurry. Hernando County.

col'-buckin', kol'-breakin': *n.* The manner in which a horse sometimes bucks when he puts his head between his knees.

conch: *n.* A descendant of the early English settlers on the lower east coast of Florida.

cow-hunting: *n.* Gathering cattle, as from swamps.

cracker: *n.* 1. The little leather thong on the end of a whip. 2. A native Floridian, particularly a backwoodsman.

crivice: *n.* A small enclosure for cattle; a corral.

cut-away and Jim swinger: *phr.* Formal clothes. Suwannee backwoods.

dobie, dogie: *n.* A motherless calf.

dus'-dark: *n.* Early sundown. Suwannee River area.

egg-sucking dog: *n.* A dog that robs the hen's nest; uncomplimentary epithet sometimes applied to human beings.

feather-legged: *adj.* Cowardly.

fin: *n.* A five-dollar bill.

fish-hawk: *n.* The osprey.

fish-head: *n.* A person from the West Florida coast.

fish-poison: *n.* A type of blood poison which gets in the flesh from a wound by a fish fin.

flint-head: *n.* The gannet.

fruit-hog: *n.* An orange picker.

gen-tul-men: *interj.* An exclamation of surprise, particularly of agreeable surprise. Hernando County.

gen-tul-frost: *interj.* An exclamation of surprise or dismay. Hernando County.

goat: *n.* A low-geared truck used for heavy hauling in fields and groves.

grampus: *n.* A large scorpion found under trash piles.

green corn, the: *n.* The June meeting of the Indians, when the corn is "in the milk." Participants "sing [or dance] the *green corn*."

ha, gals: *interj.* A cattleman's call to straying cattle.

high-button-shoe-boy: *n.* A person from West Florida. Suwannee backwoods expression.

hoa: *interj.* A cattleman's call to push the herd along. The precise meaning is often conveyed by the tone.

hull: *n.* A saddle. Cowboy speech.

humpin': *n.* The bowing, or humping, of the horse's back when he bucks.

hush puppies: *n.* Small cakes of fried corn-bread.

Indian runner: *n.* A Brahman cow in Florida.

iron-head: *n.* The gannet.

jack: *n.* A Brahman cow.

jar-head: *n.* A mule.

lammin' load: *n.* A large amount of food taken into the body through gluttony.

mouthpiece: *n.* A lawyer.

mud-buzzard: *n.* The gannet.

mule-killer: *n.* A large scorpion found under trash piles.

one-man horse: *n.* A horse that only the owner can ride. Cowboy speech.

pacer: *n.* A cow that has become anaemic through lack of mineral content in her diet. The name is derived from the manner in which the cow walks.

play pretty: *n.* A baby's toy.

plumb good 'un: *phr.* One that is perfect, or nearly so.

pogy ['pogɪ]: *n.* A shad.

pond-water: *n.* Moonshine liquor.

pore-joe: *n.* The great blue heron.

pullet, little pullet: *n.* A young girl.

push a truck: *phr.* To drive a truck in hauling logs, fruit, and the like.

relic: *n.* A saddle that is too old and weak to put on a bucking horse.

ring-tailed snorter: *n.* A person with a high temper and generally obnoxious disposition.

roun' en roun': *phr.* The manner in which a horse sometimes bucks, moving in a circle with a diameter of about fifteen feet.

santa-pee: *n.* The small scorpion found in decaying wood.

sassafracks: *n.* Sassafras.

scoggin: *n.* Any pond bird. For an interesting discussion of the word *scoggin*, see W. L. McAtee's note, *American Speech*, XX (1945), p. 230.

scroncher: *n.* A scorpion.

sea greens: *n.* A small, tender green vine which grows on sandy beaches. When cooked, it tastes much like mustard.

shiner: *n.* A shad.

short: *adj.* Without money.

skylarkin' around: *phr.* Having a good time and neglecting one's work.

sky-winding, knock something or **someone:** *phr.* To knock toward the sky.

square-head: *n.* A Swede.

Suwannee River chicken: *n.* A fresh water turtle.

swamp cabbage: *n.* The edible part of the bud of the palmetto palm.

sweepin' trot, in a: *phr.* In a big hurry.

tearing one's shirt: *phr.* Extremely impatient.

throwing melons: *phr.* Loading melons on trucks.

thousand-legger: *n.* The millipede.

toad-floater: *n.* A downpour of rain.

tribe: *n.* A family.

truth-careless: *n.* An untruth.

twine: *n.* Lariat or lasso. The cowboy will yell, "Throw that *twine* and screw it down." He means, "Lasso that animal and wind the rope around the pommel of the saddle to take up the slack."

whiskey and branch water: *phr.* A Suwannee backwoods drink.

whip 'n spur, under: *phr.* Under pressure to get something done.

wool hat boy: *n.* A person from West Florida.

wyomi ['waɪomɪ]: *n.* Intoxicating liquor.

B. SAYINGS

All right for a sittin' but not for a spell. Satisfactory for occasional, but not for continuous, use.

Bear 'em to the right. 1. Instruction passed from one cowpuncher to another while they are driving cattle. 2. Greeting of one cowpuncher to another when they meet each other on the street. It is the equivalent of "How are you?"

Not as **big** as a washing of soap after a hard day's washing. Said of a person small in stature.

If he had half a **brain,** he'd be a half-wit. Suwannee River witticism.

I'm so **broke** that if a railroad system cost a quarter, I couldn't buy a handful of spikes. Suwannee River self-depreciation.

I'm so **broke** that if all the lumber in the world cost a nickel, I couldn't afford a toothpick. Suwannee River self-depreciation.

A **bushel** and a peck and some in a gourd. Answer to the question, "Do you love me?" Hernando County.

So **busy** his coat has been standing straight out all day. Suwannee River saying.

So **busy** my feets been in the road all day. Suwannee River backwoods speech.

That's some **come-off**! An odd way to behave, or an unfortunate occurrence. Hernando County.

Crawl your frame. To give one a beating or thrashing.

Draw in your horns. Advice to a person who has become angry without good reason.

As **drunk** as a skunk in a moonshine still. Suwannee backwoods simile.

Dry up! A command to get quiet, to hush up.

She could **eat** a pumpkin to the hollow through a crack in a board fence. Description of a buck-toothed girl. Suwannee River backwoods speech.

Eating high off the hog. Living in luxury.

Ain't **feelin'** so-many-delicious. Description of one's depressed feelings. Suwannee River backwoods speech.

Fine as frog hair. Hernando County simile in answer to "How are you?"

Fine as split silk. Hernando County simile in answer to "How are you?"

Forty miles behind. Used with reference to an accumulation of work.

Froggin' around in the rain. Prowling around in the rain. Hernando County.

If I had a **gal** as pretty as that, I'd plow her to death just to watch her walk. Suwannee backwoods compliment.

Grinning like a mule eating briars. Suwannee backwoods simile.

Happy as a dead hog [or as dead pigs] in the sunshine. Suwannee backwoods simile.

Ain't been so **happy** since the ole sow ate my mother-in-law. Suwannee backwoods speech.

Hol' 'em up; hol' 'em close; 'hol 'em, boys; hol' 'em tight. Instructions to cowboys to hold the cattle close in, or to hold them still.

Hot as the seven brass hinges of hell. Suwannee backwoods simile.

Hot as a nigger in hell writing a love-letter and trying to spell *Chattahoochee*. Suwannee backwoods simile.

So **hungry** that I can see biscuits walking around on crutches. Suwannee backwoods simile.

So **hungry** I could eat a sow and seven pigs and run a boar hog a mile. Suwannee backwoods simile.

As **hungry** as a she-wolf suckling nine to the side. Suwannee backwoods simile.

Knee-high to a jack-rabbit. Descriptive epithet referring usually to one's childhood.

As **lazy** as a hound-dog-puppy. Suwannee backwoods simile.

Can **lie** faster than a dog can trot. Hernando County simile.

Livin' in hog heaven. Suwannee backwoods simile for lush living.

Livin' in high cotton. Suwannee backwoods simile for lush living.

Look out, Brindy! The cowboy's call to a straying cow.

Looks like a sheep-killing dog. Said of a person with a guilty expression.

Lord love a duck! Suwannee backwoods expression of surprise.

So **low** he could crawl under the belly of a snake without touching him. Suwannee backwoods simile.

Lyin' out with the dry cattle. Staying out late at night with the unmarried set.

I were so **mad** I just lay there and drunk snuff. Suwannee backwoods expression.

I was so **mad** I could chew up nails and spit up tacks. Suwannee backwoods expression.

He was so **mad** he didn't care if to spit or go blind. Suwannee backwoods expression.

Naked as a jaybird. Suwannee backwoods simile.

A **nose** like an over-ripe pumpkin. Suwannee backwoods simile.

A **nose** like a regular yaller squash. Suwannee backwoods simile.

Nose stuck in the air like a goose looking for a hole in the fence. Suwannee backwoods simile.

As **ornery** as an old suck-egg-dog. Suwannee backwoods simile.

Pleasant as a basket of chips. Hernando County simile.

Pop your whip. Do as you please; it makes no difference to me.

No matter what you **say**, hit don't make no nevermin', I ain't a goin' to listen to you. Suwannee backwoods expression.

Sit down and blow awhile. To rest and catch one's breath.

Smell him forty miles against the wind. Said of a person who needs a bath, or of anyone with an offensive odor.

Didn't have a **snowball's** chance in hell. Suwannee backwoods expression.

Stem-windin' good 'un [or **stem-winder**]. Some event or person that is especially noteworthy or exciting.

Teach your granny to lap ashes. Usually said to a child who tries to correct an older person.

MINORCAN DIALECT WORDS IN
ST. AUGUSTINE, FLORIDA

LILLIAN FRIEDMAN

St. Augustine, Florida

In 1768 about twelve hundred natives of the Mediterranean island of Minorca were brought to the east coast of Florida to work in sugar and indigo crops. They were colonized at New Smyrna. There they underwent many hardships, not the least of which was oppressive treatment by their taskmasters. In 1777 many of them escaped northward to St. Augustine and were assigned lands in the northern part of that city. Many of their descendants live in that area today and employ certain expressions peculiar to their own group. Some of these expressions, chiefly epithets, and their significations are as follows:

babowa [bə'baυwə]: *n.* A dull-witted, stupid person.

bofia ['bofιə]: *n.* An expressionless face; a deadpan.

bomba ['bombə]: *n.* A sleepy-head.

brusha ['bruʃə]: *n.* A person with a heavy head of hair.

brutuzus ['brʌtəzəs]: *n.* An action considered in bad taste.

bunoula [bə'naυlə]: *n.* A dull-witted, stupid person.

bustara [bus'tɑrə]: *n.* A falsehood; a lie.

caraplanta [kɑrə'plɑntə]: *n.* A flat-face.

chopa ['tʃopə]: *n.* A sunfish; a person resembling a sunfish.

cuzishaw? [kəzi'ʃaυ]: *poly.* Who's that?

ficusa [fɪ'kʌsə]: *n.* Sensation a person has when he is so hungry that his stomach growls. "I've got the *ficusa.*"

figúra (fɪ'gurə]: *n.* Thankfulness. "I've got the *figura.*"

lawca ['lɔkə]: *adj.* Crazy.

naschata [nɑz'kɑtə]: *n.* A flat-nose.

teleganostanaza (tə'legənostə'nɑzə]: *n.* A stupid person.

THE AMERICAN DIALECT SOCIETY

Membership in the Society is conferred upon any person interested in the activities of the Society. Dues are $2.00 a year for persons or institutions. Members receive free all publications. The price of any issue when purchased separately will depend upon the production cost of the issue.

The *Publication of the American Dialect Society* is issued twice a year, in April and November.